BOOT STRAP
ENTREPRENEUR

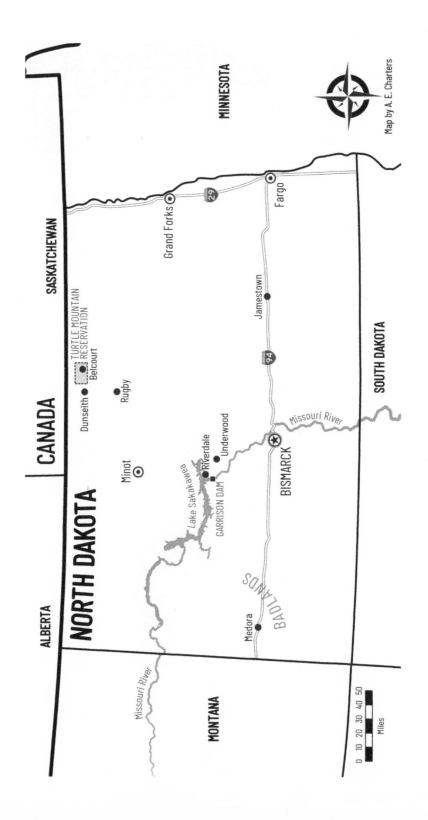

Map by A. E. Charters

BOOT STRAP ENTREPRENEUR

How Grit, Faith, and Help from a
Chippewa Tribe Built a Technology Company

A Business Memoir

John Miller

John Miller, Shoreview, MN

Published 2022
Printed in the United States of America

ISBN 979-8-9866156-2-2 (hardcover)
ISBN 979-8-9866156-1-5 (paperback)
ISBN 979-8-9866156-0-8 (e-book)
ISBN 979-8-9866156-3-9 (audiobook)

Library of Congress Control Number: 2022914377

Coauthored by Christina Schweighofer
Book Design: KarrieRoss.com
Cover Photo: North Dakota by Rick Bohn,
US Fish and Wildlife Service
(https://creativecommons.org/licenses/by/2.0/deed.en); TMC
core memory by Alan Kallmeyer, North Dakota State University
Editing by Carol J. Amato
Other photographs, unless otherwise stated, are from the
author's collection.

For my family

*To the next generation
of entrepreneurs*

Table of Contents

Part A:

Know Yourself

1.

Joining a Start-Up in St. Paul

I WAS TEN YEARS into my career at the UNIVAC division of Sperry Rand, where I worked on shipboard and airborne computers for the Navy, when a group of colleagues asked me to join their start-up, Atron Corporation. The invitation surprised me, but I had respect for the electrical engineers behind the new venture. Finley "Mac" McLeod, Bob Bergman, and Bob Burkeholder were brilliant computer designers, as was Hy Osofsky, with whom I am still in touch. I quickly agreed to their offer, thereby trading a management position with an established company and pioneer in the computer industry for the uncertainty of a new business.

My wife, Pat, supported my decision—until a neighbor came to our house in St. Paul, Minnesota, with a pair of pants for our son, Mike, that her own boy had outgrown. "Why are people sending hand-me-downs our way?" she asked me later that day. "Are you doing something that I should be worried about?"

Like hundreds of other people launching start-ups, we at Atron had high aspirations. Our goal was to create our own product line of data-entry stations and compete with companies like IBM. Our first customer, right from the beginning, was Mohawk Data Sciences (MDS). Located on the East Coast and also a recent UNIVAC spinoff, MDS had developed an advanced data-entry system that used magnetic tape instead of punched cards to record data. Our contract with them included the design and manufacture of a computer that relied on core memory, which, back then, was still the industry standard for computer memory. My role at Atron was the same as at UNIVAC; I was responsible for the manufacturing department.

IN 1971, Louis Amyotte, a technician in the core-memory group and member of the Turtle Mountain Band of Chippewa in my home state, North Dakota, approached me. "Making core memory is just like beadwork," he said. "Our women do that well, and there's a lot of unemployment on the reservation. Why don't you ship some of the work up there?"

Shifting our production of core memory away from St. Paul to an American Indian reservation five hundred miles from St. Paul was a bold idea. But Louis had a point.

Core memory was a labor-intensive product, consisting of printed-wiring boards made of epoxy glass, tiny doughnut-shaped ferrite beads (aka cores) and wires as thin as a human hair that had to be threaded through the cores in a grid pattern. The key to producing a high-quality, reliable product was precision. Since the assembly had to be done by hand and required exceptional dexterity and eyesight, I could certainly understand why the process would remind Louis of beadwork.

On the other hand, core memory was already a doomed technology. Sooner or later, the electronic chip, which was invented in 1958, was going to replace it.

Creating a new plant for a dying product would have seemed like folly to most people, and I was admittedly doubtful of Louis's suggestion. There was also a political problem. In recent years, tensions between the Native American population and the government in Washington, DC, had increased, with activists occupying federally owned property to draw attention to the many challenges reservations faced. And tribes were often suspicious of white people coming in with government support and big promises that didn't materialize. Stories of such ventures failing because the investor proved to be a shyster abounded.

Willing to at least explore Louis's idea, I visited Belcourt, the seat of the Turtle Mountain Chippewa, as I was en route to celebrating Easter in my hometown, Underwood, North Dakota. After talking with the tribe's representatives, I increasingly liked Louis's suggestion.

The reservation, which covers six miles by twelve miles and is the most densely populated in the country, already featured a building a few miles west of Belcourt that could serve as a manufacturing plant. Originally constructed for the production of Chippewa authentics that the tribe had wanted to sell to tourists, it had a footprint of 3,500 square feet and was being used as a commodity disbursement center after the souvenirs enterprise had failed. Jim Henry, who was the tribal chairman, assured me that we could use the facility for free.

Our plant, in the background, on the Turtle Mountain Reservation.

I also learned that the Tribal Council, the Bureau of Indian Affairs (BIA), and the Economic Development Administration (EDA) would support a three-month-long training of the workers from the reservation in Atron's factory in St. Paul and provide them with housing while they were in the Twin Cities.

The Turtle Mountain Chippewa are a community of Ojibwe and Métis people. The Ojibwe, who once occupied one-third of what is now the State of North Dakota, are one of the largest indigenous people in the country, and their language is spoken by over fifty thousand people in Canada and the US. The Métis are people of mixed indigenous and French ancestry with their own language, traditions, and music.

I remember saying to Jim that the Turtle Mountain Reservation had a different atmosphere from others in North Dakota, like Standing Rock.

"We're Chippewa," he said. "We're probably as much French as Indian. We aren't fighters, we're lovers."

IN THE END, I decided we should take the Chippewa's offer. If they delivered on their promises, Atron would be bringing work to an underserved area while also reducing the cost for its core-memory production. If the tribe didn't deliver, little would be lost.

After convincing Atron's top management of the plan, I was responsible for the plant start-up, and during the summer of 1971, fifteen people from Belcourt came to the Twin Cities for training in core-memory stringing and soldering. Bob Wilmot, a recent mechanical-engineering graduate from North Dakota State University (NDSU), my alma mater, was hired to learn about core-memory production along with the trainees. He would then return with them to North Dakota and oversee our operations in the new plant.

Over the next two years, employment grew to seventy, and eventually we even added people from outside the reservation to work in the plant.

2.

Early Lessons in Underwood

IN HINDSIGHT, Pat's—or at least our neighbor's—concerns about my joining a brand-new company seem more valid than they did to me at the time.

Starting a business is always risky, and back in the early 1970s, the short- and long-term survival chances of new enterprises were the same as now. About four in five new businesses make it through their first year, one in two lasts at least five years, and only one in five reaches the twenty-year mark.

I may not have been aware of these numbers when I joined Atron. But as a husband and father of three children, I knew I wanted us to be successful.

Thirty-three years old, I also felt confident of my own capabilities as a manager. In the years leading up to Atron, I had shown commitment; a positive, faith-based attitude; competitiveness; and a high tolerance for frustration. I had taken responsibility as a student at NDSU in Fargo; learned to lead as an ROTC member and in a Field Artillery Officers Basic course in Fort Sill, Oklahoma, where I was trained to be a forward observer; and progressed at UNIVAC from mechanical design engineer to manufacturing manager. Mentors had inspired me always to do my best, business owners for whom I worked in Fargo and Underwood had served as excellent role models, and from my folks and other people in my hometown, I knew the value of community and hard work.

WHEN I WAS BORN in 1935, Underwood had a population of about five hundred. Located just one hundred miles south of the Canadian border and halfway between Bismarck and Minot on US 83, it's the kind of place where you'll find a grocery store, a bank, and a post office in the same block downtown, and where everybody knows everyone.

Underwood, North Dakota, in 1953. (Photo courtesy of Ron Fandrick.)

My father, Ernie, was born in Minnesota to Swedish immigrants but spent most of his childhood and youth in Sweden, only to return to the US by himself at age seventeen. He settled with relatives in North Dakota, learned English, served in World War I, and trained as a machinist. By the time my folks met, he had moved to Underwood, where he worked at a garage that sold Ford cars and farm equipment.

During the war, if a machine broke down, you couldn't just order a replacement part because all manufacturing was geared toward supporting the troops. Instead, Dad created replacement parts himself, developing a solid reputation for his skills as a machinist.

I was always proud when I heard farmers say, "You should see the part that Ernie made to keep my tractor going."

After school, I sometimes walked down to the shop and watched him. Usually, I'd find him humming a song as he worked, a hand-rolled cigarette hanging out of his mouth. The conditions were often terrible. In the spring, when the snow melted and the roof leaked, there was water everywhere. Hours at the garage were long, fifty-five or sixty a week.

Times were tough back then. Most of Underwood had no running water until city water and sewer were installed after the war ended. Our home had an outhouse in the back, and on Saturday nights, after my parents had drawn freezing-cold water from a well and heated it on a stove, we would go to an attached back shed to take a bath in a metal tub.

My mother, Sophie, had to soak Dad's greasy clothes in water with bits of soap that she cut from a bar before sticking them in an old wringer washing machine in the basement. There were no clothes dryers. In the winter, our washed clothes hung outside and were frozen stiff and then brought in to dry on a collapsible rack in front of a register from the gravity furnace.

Keeping the furnace going was Dad's job. In the morning, when the coal-fed fire had died down, he was in the cellar, shaking the grates to get the ashes off. The whole house trembled, but the fire always rekindled.

My mom, who grew up about one hundred miles from Underwood, in Kenmare, was fourteen years younger than Dad. Half-Danish, half-Swedish, she attended summer sessions at Minot State Teachers College so she could teach grades one through eight at a small country school. Then she met him and started a family. During World War II, she took a job with the local post office. Like in other places, labor was scarce because many residents had left to serve overseas or taken government positions in Washington, DC.

The postmaster told her, "Sophie, if you don't come and work for the post office, we can't keep it open. There's no one else to do the job."

The position was a godsend for the family because it came with benefits, something Dad didn't receive at the garage. Since Mom always had the early-morning shift, friends of hers would sometimes stop by to help get us kids off to school. They were a helpful bunch.

After returning from work in the mornings, Mom still had all the housework and a plant and vegetable garden that she tended to with help from Dad. Carrots and potatoes were stored in a root cellar in hopes that they would last us through the winter, and except for flour, meat, spices, and sugar, there wasn't much shopping going on. Mom did the cooking and baked bread, cakes, and pies for our family, with eggs from chickens in the backyard barn and pen. Plus, she had us children; Colleen was born just fifteen months after me, and Sonja came in 1942.

While Dad spent more time listening than talking, Mom was a social, outgoing person. Having come to Underwood as an outsider, she was nevertheless well integrated in the community and raised my sisters and me always to be friendly. Her motto, "If you don't have time to say hello, you're too busy," became a guiding principle for my own life and business.

BOTH MY PARENTS valued honesty, and both worked very hard to provide for the family's basic needs. Neither had a degree, and their biggest goal was for their three kids to finish college without a pile of debt. Growing up, if my two younger sisters and I had wants, we usually had to work for them. Our folks were weaning us off.

I was still in grade school when I first tried my luck at sales, with greeting cards as merchandise. Through a newspaper ad, I had found a place where I could order packets of Christmas, sympathy, and birthdays cards. If Mom had friends over for coffee, I might say to them, "Christmas is coming. Do you want Christmas cards?"

Each box of a dozen cards cost me sixty cents, and I'd sell them for one dollar. It was the highest-margin venture I ever experienced.

My first paid job was delivering the *Minot Daily News* and the *Minneapolis Sunday Tribune*. They came on a bus that traveled the 120 miles from Bismarck to Minot in the morning and back at night, often carrying not just the papers but supplies and parts for stores and garages. We didn't have UPS and FedEx back then. If you needed something quickly, the bus drivers, who soon became popular with the locals, helped.

With my sisters and folks in 1946.

One of my stops on the paper route was the house of Christine Johnson, a neighbor who occasionally came over in the mornings to help get us kids off to school while Mom worked the early shift at the post office. When I arrived with the paper, Christine would ask me in for a glass of milk with cookies. In the winter, when it became extremely cold, other people did the same. "Come on in, Tip! Come on in!" they would say, using the nickname that my grandfather assigned to me. (As the story goes, he thought that I looked like a rooster. In Swedish that's *tupp*, which is pronounced similar to the English word *tip*.)

My other jobs included washing windshields at the Texaco station, working at construction sites, and selling popcorn and operating the film projector at the movie theater. At the local pharmacy, which was owned and run by NDSU alum Percy Evander, I was a janitor and stock boy and a soda jerk when times were busy, like after ball games.

I always felt that there was something secretive about Percy's work and in the way he counted pills; labeled vials, bottles, and boxes; and concocted salves and suppositories with cocoa butter.

Percy instilled in me the relevant code of ethics.

"Tip," he'd say, "what goes on in the pharmacy stays in the pharmacy."

Evander's pharmacy was old-style. Some men would sit at the counter for long periods of time smoking a cigarette, drinking coffee for five cents a cup including refills, and talking sports and politics. Others would order ice cream sodas and malts from the fountain. The recipe for an ice cream soda, or float, was two "squirts" of flavored syrup, then add a scoop of ice cream, stir the syrup and ice cream, mix everything while adding soda water, then add another scoop of ice cream and more soda to fill the glass. I made lots of root beer and strawberry floats.

One afternoon, one of my favorite people in town, young World War II veteran Shag Mac Phee, came in with his wife, Lucille. Propped on stools at the counter, they had just started licking their cones when Percy's wife, Larry, asked Lucille to join her in the prescription room. The women started talking, the ice cream began melting, and soon Shag was sitting there licking two cones.

"Have you been eating my ice cream?" Lucille asked as she stepped out from the back room.When Shag said yes, she grabbed her cone and stuck it right in his face. There he was, wearing a big smile and licking ice cream off his chin as best he could.

That a marriage could be so playful was new to me. My folks loved to laugh, but they didn't tease each other in this way.

Pursuing different opportunities as a young kid allowed me to hone my people skills, work under different bosses, and learn from them as they went about their daily work. I was surrounded by entrepreneurs with gas stations, hardware stores, car dealerships, and grocery and clothing stores. What I knew from working for them was that they were good people and independent. Of course, I had no idea how difficult their lives were.

I WAS STILL A KID when my willingness to take on a challenge combined with a desire to see new places earned me two memorable trips. The first one was my prize for signing up a certain number of new customers for the Minneapolis Sunday paper. Taking me on the Northern Pacific passenger train to Minneapolis, it included a tour of the city and tickets to a hockey game. Hockey wasn't popular in North Dakota, so I wasn't much interested in that part. But the city, with its tall buildings—holy mackerel! I had never seen anything like it. At the time, the thirty-two-story Foshay Tower was the tallest skyscraper between Chicago and the West Coast. I still remember feeling awed as I stood in front of it, looking up.

As a high school freshman, I saw an opportunity for another trip. The year was 1950, and the Boy Scouts of America were planning their second National Jamboree. While the first one, in 1937, had taken place in Washington, DC, this one was to be held in Valley Forge, Pennsylvania.

The cost for the three-week trip and train ride to attend the Jamboree was $250. It was a lot of money, but my troop offered a subsidy: the Boy Scout who earned the most merit badges would receive $100 toward the trip.

People, in general, tended to be supportive of the merit badge program, which qualifies Boy Scouts for the ranks of Star, Life, and Eagle. By requiring that Scouts serve in positions of responsibility and perform community service, it allows them to develop leadership skills and explore interests, passions, and potential vocations.

I went to my folks and said, "If I win this competition, I get $100 off the $250 that the trip to Valley Forge costs. Do you think you could come up with the $150 that's still needed?"

They said yes. I think they understood it as another opportunity on my journey to independence.

Having secured their financial support for the Jamboree, I got to work. My Boy Scout book listed the qualifications for all the different merit badges. I'd pick a badge, work to pass it, and then select another one.

Shag Mac Phee and another World War II veteran and member of what has become known as the Greatest Generation, Art Turner, were often my go-to people when I needed help. They must have been about thirty at that time, lived across the alley from us, and had both married into the Henricks family that owned the garage and Ford dealership where Dad worked. Transplants from the coasts, Shag and Art, I believe, had never been anywhere close to North Dakota before moving to Underwood, and they knew little about agriculture. But they were smart and fun to be around.

While Dad, who was a member of the American Legion, worked in the shop, these two young veterans were out front selling cars and farm machinery, scheduling shop work, and handling the finances. After school, I would visit them and say, "I want to win this merit badge competition so that I can go on a trip to Valley Forge."

Shag and Art showed some interest and helped a bit, but, at the same time, they kept poking fun at me. As I look back, I sometimes wonder whether they perceived me as a pest; I was certainly aggressive in pursuing that adventure.

I undertook the three-week trip to Pennsylvania, in June 1950, with my friend Cliff Thompson. Two Scouts among forty-five thousand from all over the country, he and I were lumped in with other Scouts from North Dakota. We set up our tents on the historical encampment grounds where, in the winter of 1777–78, General George Washington turned the American Revolutionary War around by unifying the army.

Being in an area of historical significance and in the company of thousands of enthusiastic Boy Scouts was already an adventure. The timing of the trip added to its significance.

Overall, the years following World War II were a time of great patriotism. Our guys had gotten the job done and come back home, making everyone feel proud. Women who had worked for the government and in industries supporting the war effort also came home, some of them towing love interests from out of state. Families were reunited and romantic relationships rekindled.

I was only ten years old when the bombs dropped in Japan, finally ending the war in the Pacific for the US. But I, too, could feel the excitement and everyone's eagerness to move on with their civilian lives. People got married, had children, and built houses. New jobs were created, especially in the construction industry. And the American flag flew everywhere, even in our churches, where it was placed near the pulpit, with a Christian flag on the other side.

The Jamboree—the theme that year was "Strengthen Liberty"—was a huge national event that impressed me immensely. Only two days before its official kick-off, news had reached us of the Korean People's Army crossing the border into South Korea. Now, with a new war seeming imminent, Cliff and I saw President Harry Truman, who spoke at the event, drive by in his motorcade. We were there for a July 4th celebration with spectacular fireworks and for an address by General "Ike" Eisenhower, the national hero who led the invasions of Africa and Normandy in World War II. From that time on, I knew that I liked Ike, who soon afterward became president.

Cliff and I visited several historical sites during our trip. In Philadelphia, we went to see the cracked Liberty Bell and the house where Betsy Ross sewed the first American flag. In Washington, DC, we saw the Capitol, the Washington Monument, and the Lincoln Memorial.

Boy Scouts from North Dakota at the Valley Forge Jamboree.
I am in the middle row, the fourth kid from the right.

The Lincoln Memorial has always been special to me because of the inscriptions on the walls, the Gettysburg Address in particular. But the site that impressed me most back in 1950—and that continues to do so—is the Tomb of the Unknown Soldier at Arlington Cemetery with the changing of the guard. Talk about precision drills! The soldiers are there during hurricanes and storms, doing their duty. They show respect with every step, impeccable uniforms, and an unflappable demeanor.

For Cliff, who was eighteen, our East Coast trip was sometimes stressful. The son of the banker in Underwood, he had lost a brother in World War II, and now the Korean War was in the news. We didn't have TV at home, but tents throughout the camp that served as gathering spaces with refreshments and treats had large screens. There was talk of men his age being drafted. Cliff couldn't help but wonder whether he would be called to serve. It was a tough time for him to be away from home.

Back from the Jamboree, Cliff and I wrote a front-page article for the *Underwood News*, telling of our great experience. Some weeks later, I was in for a little surprise. The troop, which had paid the promised one hundred dollars toward my trip, was now asking me to help raise funds for the replenishing of their bank account.

"Since you won the deal," they said, "would you help earn it back?"

The fundraising effort that our Scout committee came up with involved a magazine salesman, whose earnings were going to benefit the troop. My task was to introduce the guy to people in Underwood so that he could pitch them.

Not everybody liked being approached in this way. One farmer was out in a field when we met him. As we drove up, he stopped his tractor, climbed down from the driver's seat, and said, "Hi, Tip. How are you? And who's your guy? What does he do?"

"He sells magazines."

"Tip," the farmer said, "I don't want to talk to him. You take him and get off my property!"

Looking back, I probably would have said the same.

A COUPLE OF MONTHS after the Jamboree, a few other boys from the area and I were inducted into one of the Boy Scout honor societies, the Order of the Arrow (OA). The initiation took place on the banks of the Little Missouri River. It was after nightfall, and our campfires glowed in the background.

Our initiator was an OA member named John Baumgartner. He was a football star at Bismarck High School, and I already knew him from Valley Forge where he and other OAs had been tasked with responsibilities like directing traffic and looking after younger Scouts. I remember him leading a bunch of us North Dakota kids around the encampment singing the "Minnesota Rouser." To us, this felt strange, but he had already signed on with the University of Minnesota's football team.

During the initiation, I watched as John raised his hand for each of the boys lined up in front of me and dropped it onto their shoulders. When it was my turn, I felt his hand come down with such force that it seemed like I was sinking two inches into the ground.

Part of the initiation ceremony was a test where the Scout leaders blindfolded us inductees and led everyone out into the prairie with nothing but a sleeping bag. They dropped us off, one by one, with instructions to leave the blindfolds on until they had left.

As I unrolled my sleeping bag, I looked up to the night sky for orientation. Aware of the position of the moon during the preceding initiation ceremony, I understood which direction I was facing. *If I go back that way*, I thought, already feeling hungry for breakfast, *I will be okay*.

Being an OA and a bit older than the rest of the troop, I later became an assistant scoutmaster. One time, when our regular scoutmaster had a conflict, Father Thomas Dolan led the troop on a camping trip instead. The pastor of St. Bonaventure's, the Catholic parish in Underwood, he would often travel with us kids to sports games and on Boy Scout outings. On this camping trip, I was an assistant, and Father Dolan and I shared a tent. After lights out, he asked me to hold up the lantern for him so that he could do his nightly reading.

When I asked him about it, he said, "It's just something I have to do, Tip."

Father Dolan was a great guy, but it turned out that the priesthood was not for him. He later laid down the collar for marriage.

THE BEST WAY to describe my religious background is probably as Methodist-Lutheran-Baptist. Mom, whose faith was strong, was Baptist, but, in Underwood, that congregation spoke German. Dad was baptized Lutheran, but the local Augustana Lutheran congregation spoke Swedish. The Methodist church was the only English-speaking Protestant congregation left, so that's where we went.

As a member of the Methodist Youth Fellowship in Underwood, I came to appreciate the Methodists' love for music as an expression of faith. The power of hymns like "He Walks with Me, and He Talks with Me," "I'll Walk with God," and "He Leadeth Me" has stayed with me and often felt sustaining in times of crisis.

The summer of my junior year, a few men belonging to the Gideons, the evangelical Christian association known for its hotel-room Bibles, volunteered one Sunday to substitute for the Lutheran pastor. Shag Mac Phee, who was our Sunday school teacher, preached, and another Gideon, one of the Schafer boys, led the congregations in prayers. Our high school boys' quartet provided the special music. Together, we held services at three churches.

During the weeks leading up to this Sunday, we had seen some exceptionally dry weather that left farmers fearing for their crops. Our first service took us to Birka Lutheran Church located south of Underwood, where Schafer prayed for rain. As we traveled on to Augustana in town, it cooled off, and there was a drizzle. Our prayers changed; we thanked the Lord for rain and said we hoped for more. By the time we left Malcolm up north, it was pouring so hard that the unpaved road turned to mud, and we barely made it home.

The local farmers breathed relief. I saw my faith fortified.

Teachers also helped strengthen the foundation that my folks had built. Ardis Hodenfield, who taught English, liked to remind us to "always remember the little folks."

"We're all the same," she'd say.

Our music and mathematics teacher, Philip Hetland, was a veteran with a small frame who always spoke softly. He was a surprisingly good boxer. A couple of my classmates learned this the hard way when they set up a boxing ring on the stage of the gymnasium and invited Hetland to a bout.

Erling "Ben" Thomson, who was big, said after the match, "I thought Hetland would never stop. He didn't tell us that he boxed in the Navy."

It was an early lesson in stereotyping. How we perceive people may have little to do with who they are.

Hetland, who later became a professor at NDSU, was a strong Christian or, as he liked to say, a follower of Jesus. As our teacher, he encouraged hard work and often inquired about our position on topics ranging from politics to religion. "Where are you on this?" he would say. If he thought our answer was out of line, his response was "Do you need to change your course here?"

Years later, on nighttime trips from St. Paul to the Chippewa reservation, I often found myself singing a song that Hetland taught us in boys' choir. It's called "Stout Hearted Men," and the version that I learned starts with the lines "You, who have dreams, if you act they will come true. Would you turn your dreams to a fact, it's up to you. If you have the will and the spirit, never fear: it will see you through."

If the night was clear and I was getting close to the plant, the northern lights ahead of me would light up the whole world as I sang.

3.

A Haphazard Path to College and Engineering

WHILE THERE WERE clearly times in my life where I stumbled into decisions rather than planning things out—my path to college is an example—I always gave it my best shot once a choice was made. The way I see it, once you're in, you're in.

My journey to college started one late-summer evening in 1953, when I went roller-skating with a girl from nearby Riverdale, Sharon Hartl, and we happened to meet my friend Johnny Busch with his date. Over burgers, Johnny shared with us that he was leaving for Taylor University in Upland, Indiana, the next morning.

Sharon, who was one year younger than I, turned to me. "Aren't you going to college?"

"Yes, I am."

"Don't you realize that most kids have already left?"

"You should come with me," Johnny said. "I'll give you a ride."

When I got home that night and told my folks that I was going to college with Johnny, Dad objected. "What are you talking about?"

It was an unusual display of resistance on his part, but Mom, calling the shots, turned him around. "Taylor is a fine Christian college," she said. "It'll be good for him."

I packed my bag—only to tell Johnny, when he arrived at

my home in the morning, he'd have to make the one-thousand-mile trip to Upland alone. Something about Taylor just didn't feel right.

Meanwhile, Mom was out in the driveway, chatting with Phil Hetland. He suggested that I attend his alma mater, Concordia College in Moorhead, Minnesota.

"It's a good school," he said, "and maybe he can get into the choir. They have a trip to Sweden coming up."

Boy, that resonated with me!

Music has been a part of my life for as long as I can remember. While a certain talent probably came down from Dad's side—his father was a cantor and an organist in the church in Sweden—it was Mom's initiative that kept me and my sisters practicing.

In my early years, Mom would grab a hymnal, pick a song, and instruct us to sing along as she played the spinet. Later, she had me take piano lessons from Judy Hepper, the wife of the local dentist. While I didn't last long with piano lessons, I did get far enough to play most of "Beautiful Dreamer" by heart.

My biggest early musical influence came from Marie Vonderheide, who volunteer-led the Methodist Youth Fellowship. The mother of three, Jerry, Jim, and Jean, and an exceptional pianist and musician, she had us singing when we were sopranos. Along with other boys, we continued to practice into high school, where I sang bass in a quartet. As my voice developed, I eventually became comfortable doing solo work.

In high school, I also played the sousaphone, a relative of the better-known tuba. Back then, most of us kids were more interested in the trumpet because Louis Armstrong and the Harry James Orchestra were popular. Donna Anderson, Jerry Johnson, Cliff Thompson, Jim Sayler, Jerry Vonderheide, and I were all trumpeters. I switched after the only tuba player in our high school band graduated and the band director asked me to replace her. On Saturday nights, when the stores were open and the farmers came to town, we played German music downtown, with lots of polkas, and people sometimes danced to them. I enjoyed all this, in part because you can really blast out on a tuba. But the instrument I stuck with was my voice.

When Phil Hetland, back in our driveway, mentioned that possible trip to Sweden with the college choir, I was sold on Concordia. I could already see myself visiting my grandparents' home country in the company of peers who enjoyed singing as much as I did.

But I had a question of Mr. Hetland. "I'm not Lutheran. Do they take Methodists?"

"No problem," he said. "I hear they are accepting Catholics now, so you should be okay."

That same afternoon, I rushed to Moorhead in my folks' old '41 Ford—only to learn that the dormitories were already full and that I would have to live off campus with upperclassmen from Chicago, who would show me their quarters after I met them for dinner in the evening.

The choice of available classes was no less meager. Any program that still had an opening ended in -ology—and biology wasn't one of them. Even back then, I knew this much about myself: I'm a numbers guy. Yet here I was, seemingly stuck with psychology and sociology.

Sitting at dinner that evening, with a professor and the guys from Illinois, I thought about the seven hundred dollars in my bank account from my summer job with the Army Corps of Engineers. And I wondered, *How much does a private liberal arts college cost?*

After dinner, as we all stood out on the sidewalk talking, I changed my mind about college for the second time in less than twenty-four hours. "I'll see you guys," I told the others. "Thanks for dinner, but this sounds too rich to me."

Following my own intuition, I made my way across the river to Fargo. At North Dakota State University—back then it was

North Dakota Agricultural College—I tossed my bag onto an empty bunk bed in the basement of the field house and enrolled the next week.

My path to mechanical engineering was similarly haphazard. In my first few days at NDSU, I stumbled from thinking that I would study pharmacy to understanding that this meant taking chemistry and biology, which were not my favorites. When an aptitude test showed my strengths as mathematics and mechanics, I decided on architectural engineering instead. Two of my cousins were also in the engineering school, so this seemed an excellent fit. Why architecture and not mechanical or another type of engineering? Because it had the shortest sign-up line.

My final change of heart came one year later. I switched to mechanical engineering after I realized that being an architect includes creating detailed drawings that specify every kitchen tile and electrical socket. The task seemed tedious to me. In 1953, of course, computer design programs were nonexistent.

While my decision-making process with regard to college was questionable and the planning poor, to say the least, I was committed once I was in. Throughout my time at NDSU, I applied myself wholeheartedly.

Founded in 1890 as a land-grant college, i.e., with support from the federal government, NDSU was obligated by law to include military training in its curriculum and therefore has a Reserve Officers' Training Corps (ROTC) program. When I enrolled, all incoming male students were required to participate in the program for two years. I did four with the Army.

To ease the financial burden on my parents, I also found jobs on and off campus. And I contributed to the school community by serving in leadership roles in the student senate and as student body president.

4.

Once You're In, You're In

AT TIMES, I felt lonely as a freshman at NDSU. Yes, I had classes and homework for the engineering program, my part-time job, choir practice, and military classes and drills. But if my calendar was full Monday through Fridays, weekends during my first year were different. With many other students gone to visit their families nearby, the campus felt empty. Alone in a quiet dorm, I'd find myself thinking of my folks and sisters and the community that I had left behind.

Underwood is 250 miles from Fargo. Back then, the roads were all two-lane highways, and going home was not a frequent option. Fortunately, my folks had modeled perseverance. Having experienced two world wars—Dad, who was born in 1893, served in the first—and lived through the Great Depression, they just always kept going. On days where NDSU felt like the last place I wanted to be, I would remember their resilience and do the same.

Life was much easier my second year, when I became a fraternity member. Starting college, I had been dead set against pledging. Instead, I joined a local Methodist Youth Fellowship, where I met many new people from Fargo and other places bigger than Underwood. We had a weekly dinner night, and during Religious Emphasis Week, they brought in pastors for group discussions.

This was all good, but when I heard from one of my cousins about the fun he was having as a member of Sigma Alpha Epsilon, I changed my mind about fraternities.

To my surprise, the Greek system, though not quite like the military, was disciplined. Hazing, which is now outlawed, was still a big part of the pledging process. No one got hurt physically, but people's feelings may have suffered. One of the first things we had to do as pledges, in the time leading up to our initiation, was make a paddle that could be used against us if our behavior was out of line or we forgot our social graces. Failure to get out of our seats to greet and escort an alumnus might prompt a suggestion that we change our ways. As a reminder, we might get a swat with the paddle.

On Monday nights, when our fraternity sweetheart joined us for dinner, the house mother sat at the head of the table and watched how we passed the food and whether we waited to start eating until the proper time.

PAT AND I met in the concert choir at NDSU. Her singing voice was as impressive as her appearance. Tall and blonde, and a combination of German and Danish blood, she came across as a strong personality, and I liked that. What I didn't appreciate was the fact that she had a boyfriend. The two had started dating as high school kids in Moorhead, and he was now at NDSU, too.

Undeterred by her existing relationship, I still tried to see Pat as often as I could. Occasionally, I'd drop her off at her family home after a date, and his yellow Studebaker would be parked in the driveway while he talked to her mother.

I hung in there. By the time I was a junior, Pat and I were engaged. We spent time at her parents' house, dated, and laughed a lot. On one occasion, we were at a fraternity fundraiser for a charity auction where students paid to throw a pie in someone's face. Fraternity brothers had a high bid and gave the pie to Pat. She threw the pie in my face with gusto—and it was okay with me.

In situations like this, I joked with her: "Pat, I had dreams that I would find a small-size brunette who says, 'Yes, John. Yes, John. What can I do for you?' And here I am with this tall, blonde German-Dane who has a mind of her own."

On a date with Pat, circa 1957.

Pat and I complemented each other. I'm bad at memorizing and don't mind chaos. She could recall events and facts in detail and liked things to be organized. If they weren't, she would make them so.

One thing Pat couldn't stand was people leaving tasks to the last minute.

At some point, she took to calling me a procrastinator.

"Yes," I would say, "but I'm a creative procrastinator."

"What's that?"

"Well, our first option to fixing a problem may not be the best. If we wait a day or two, we'll come up with a better solution."

PAT'S BACKGROUND was very different from mine. While I grew up barely knowing of a world beyond Underwood, her family kept moving because her father, LeRoy "Bones" Larsen, was a depot agent for the railroad. Pat had lived in St. John's, Granville, and Grand Forks, all in North Dakota, and in Ada, Minnesota, before ending up in Moorhead.

For me, her family felt like a home away from home. Bones was a former athlete and Navy veteran. Covered in tattoos and blessed with a wonderful gift for storytelling, he had lost his first wife and married her sister, Lucille.

Lucille cared for Joyce, the daughter from Bones's first marriage, and was the birth mother of Pat and four other children. She doted over Bones. In the mornings, she laid out his clothing for the day, always with long sleeves to cover the tattoos. And she made sure to keep his favorite home-baked treat around. When he'd sit down at the kitchen table for coffee, he could reach back, and there was a jar full of chocolate-chip cookies.

Interestingly, it never occurred to me that I should ask Pat's parents for her hand. I somehow thought the engagement was just between her and me. We did both inform our families of our wedding date, June 14, 1957, which was the Friday of my graduation week. From what I remember, no one objected to our plans. Back then, it was quite common for people to get married at a young age.

I remember that commencement week began with our graduation and ROTC commissioning on the Monday and that my family came to Fargo for the ceremonies. Once that was over, I think I sat in my room, staring at the wall, until my best man, Syl Melroe, banged on the door.

"Tip, you need to get up. Pack your stuff and get out of here!"

"Why is that?"

"Your folks are here, the groom's dinner is tomorrow night, and you have to pick your wedding suit because you're getting married on Friday."

Just married! Pat and I walking out of Trinity Lutheran Church in Moorhead.

5.

A Country Boy in Chicago

AFTER OUR WEDDING and a short honeymoon in the Minnesota lake country, Pat and I moved to Chicago. It was a difficult transition for both of us. In a matter of three weeks, we went from single to married and from a dorm and, in her case, home-based life in Fargo-Moorhead to an apartment in a big city. I also went from student to full-time employee.

It probably didn't help that we knew our situation would be temporary. Having completed the advanced ROTC program at NDSU, I still had an obligation in the Army Reserve. Among the military obligations was a field artillery officer basic course at Fort Sill, Oklahoma, followed by six months of active duty and eight years of reserve training to ensure that we were ready when needed.

For Pat, leaving the Fargo-Moorhead area on the border of North Dakota and Minnesota meant leaving behind a large, caring family, and with it a sense of security.

She often felt lonely in Chicago. I felt out of place there.

Even riding the Elevated (now the "L" train), to the Merchandise Mart downtown, where I was a sales engineer for the Carrier Corporation, was an interesting experience for a country kid. The cars were always crowded. I had been taught to get up for women and elderly people and never knew what to make of the fact that other, much stronger-looking men just stayed in their seats.

Then there were safety concerns, something neither of us were used to. Shortly after our arrival in Chicago, Pat, who had one year of college left, arranged to tour the Armour Institute of Technology, a predecessor of the Illinois Institute of Technology. Featuring a strong home economics department, it was located on the south side of town, close to Soldier Field stadium.

The first car Pat and I bought was a used '57 Ford.

On the day of Pat's visit, I had tickets to the college all-star game against the New York Giants, and so we decided to meet at the school. She would take our 1957 Ford station wagon, and I'd go down on the Elevated.

When I told my colleagues at Carrier about my date with Pat later that day, they were shocked. "You let your beautiful young wife take the new car down there all by herself? And she's dressed up to meet the home economics teachers? John, you might never see her again."

That I should first research whether an area is safe for an attractive young woman never even occurred to me.

WHAT CONVINCED ME to leave Chicago sooner than planned was an incident not long after the all-star game. Pat's folks were in town for a few days, and one evening, we were in our apartment, watching TV on our new portable set, a wedding gift, when the police knocked.

"Your TV is too loud."

When her folks left a few days later, Pat was in tears—and I called the Army to ask about starting my basic training class earlier than planned. Not due to report until February 1958, I wanted to get the hell out of Chicago as soon as possible.

Luckily, the Army said yes, and by October, I was in Fort Sill, Oklahoma.

Pat, meanwhile, moved back in with her folks after learning that she could go back to NDSU and get her degree in a matter of two quarters.

This seemed like a good idea—but being apart was not. Pat and I talked on the phone so often and for so long that Bones, seeing the bill increase, intervened. "You need to quit talking on the telephone," he told Pat. "Or you must go to Oklahoma."

By Thanksgiving, we were together again, living in a second-story apartment in Lawton, and Pat enrolled in a university extension program that allowed her to take college classes by mail.

I made some good friends in the Army. A lot of them were from the South, where there seems to be more of a military tradition. I often found it hard to understand how these men, who were solid Christian people, might support the discriminatory laws of the Jim Crow era. But I liked them nonetheless—and they enjoyed spending time with Pat and me. Being used to bachelor's quarters, they appreciated the company of an attractive young lady as much as Pat's cooking skills.

BY THE TIME I was done with my officer training in the spring of 1958, Pat was pregnant. We briefly returned to Moorhead, and I went job hunting. It wasn't easy back then, but I lined up two interviews in Minnesota, one with the Mando Paper Company in International Falls and another with Sperry Rand's UNIVAC in St. Paul.

Pat in Fort Sill, Oklahoma, shortly after she joined me there in late 1957.

UNIVAC had risen to national fame in the presidential election of 1952, when its first big machine, the UNIVAC I, predicted General Dwight D. Eisenhower's landslide win over Adlai Stevenson. By contrast, the final Gallup poll had Stevenson winning, albeit narrowly.

I drove first to International Falls, which is in the Lake Country, and was immediately taken with the beauty of the forests—and repulsed by the smell of the paper mills. On my visit, I learned that Mando had a health program and that I would need to get a physical from a doctor in the Twin Cities before they could hire me. To me, this seemed strange. Upon my release from the service in Fort Sill, the Army doctors had checked me through to make sure that I hadn't suffered in any way in the military.

I combined my initial interview with UNIVAC with the Mando physical in St. Paul. "You have great blood pressure and eyesight," the doctor said before proceeding to check my rear end. I was used to this from the Army—or so I thought. This physician checked my prostate, something I had never experienced before. The physical, in combination with the smell of the paper mills, was too much for me. I determined then and there that I was never going to work for Mando.

The first person I met at UNIVAC was the personnel manager, Gordy Bourne, a former Marine with an impressive vocabulary of four-letter words. After lunch in the cafeteria of the famed Montgomery Ward department store, he took me over to a drafty old factory on Prior and Minnehaha, where, unbeknownst to me, computer legends like William "Bill" Norris had worked. There, I was introduced to the mechanical engineering supervisor, Earl Hanson, and taken on a tour. In the main shop, they were building a prototype computer for the Naval Tactical Data System later to be used on combat ships. This was impressive.

At the end of my visit, Hanson said, "John, can you start tomorrow?"

"Well," I said, "I have a wife up in Moorhead, and I need to get back there."

By the time I left the UNIVAC building later that day, I had a deal, with a starting salary of $108 a week. Pat and I found an apartment on Lookout Place in Columbia Heights, and she enrolled in the home economics program at the University of Minnesota to complete her degree.

6.

UNIVAC, My Training Ground

WHEN I JOINED UNIVAC, I was barely twenty-three years old and still had a lot to learn, including practical skills like staying on top of things and keeping commitments. In this area, an in-house seminar led to a breakthrough that significantly increased my efficiency. I heard that I should carry a notebook to record the events of the day, sort through my notes before leaving work in the evening, and prepare action items with priorities for the next day. In the morning, rather than wondering which task to tackle next, I could hit the ground running. These days, of course, there are apps to help people stay on track.

My task as a mechanical engineer was to support the electrical engineers in their design projects. It was creative work that often led to interesting results. At one point, John Johnson needed something more accurate than a joystick, so a tracking ball seemed to be the answer. After purchasing a cue ball at a local billiard store, I machined an aluminum block and added bearings to retain the ball in the block. I also added two potentiometers with long shafts. As it turned out, it was an upside-down mouse.

During my time at UNIVAC, computing changed at a rapid pace. In 1958, the year I joined the department, Philco introduced an all-transistor data-processing system—and this was already seen as a breakthrough. Compared to previous machines, which used vacuum tubes and took up multiple floors, the Philco Transac S-2000 model was much smaller. But it was still large enough for the sales brochure to list weight and size specifications.

Only a few years later, Martin Company created computers with integrated circuits, and computers had shrunk to the point where an advertising prospectus no longer mentioned tonnage and square footage.

By 1968, the year I left UNIVAC, the industry had gone from copper wiring to printed wiring boards and from single to multilayered printed boards. The footprint of a computer was down to the size of a filing cabinet.

Being involved in some of these shifts, I relearned at UNIVAC a lesson from my time in student leadership at NDSU: if your task includes creativity, as most tasks should because almost any operation can be improved, you must be prepared for some flack. People often believe that things are just fine the way they are, and change can, therefore, result in pushback.

Take our early transition from double to multilayered circuit boards. I wasn't the engineer on the project. One day, however, I happened to visit that group in Plant 3. They were bonding together with epoxy two double-sided boards that already had been drilled so that, in a next step, components could be added. But epoxy kept flowing into the holes, thereby blocking them, and a bunch of people with dental picks were struggling to get the holes clean.

I wondered, *Why don't we drill and plate the interconnection holes after the lamination?*

When I suggested this for my design project, the manager and engineer of the fab shop agreed to try it.

Shortly afterward, I was at my neighbor Don Lindquist's house for beer and burgers when another visitor, who worked for the printed circuit fabrication shop in Plant 3, shared his frustration over some "crazy ideas" that engineers in another department were developing. Apparently, he was referring to our project. But they went through with it, and it worked.

UNIVAC WAS, without doubt, the best training ground that a young engineer like me could find. Being with the department allowed me to follow my creative instincts, hone my NDSU-proven team-building skills, work with some of the most inventive engineers of the time, learn from a mentor, and serve my country, at least indirectly.

The focus of the UNIVAC division where I worked during half of my UNIVAC time was on satisfying the Navy's needs for countering airborne threats to its fleet. This included development of the first Naval Tactical Data System (NTDS).

The story behind the NTDS, which Captain David Boslaugh has laid out in detail,[1] starts a few years after World War II with the replacement of propeller planes by high-speed jet fighters and the need for a fast-tracking air defense management system.

Until then, battleship air defense had relied on the work of sailors, who analyzed data and relayed information in real time. They read radar blips emitted by attacking aircraft and friendly airplanes, plotted them onto a backlit Plexiglas table, calculated the speed and course of aircraft manually from successive radar blips, and wore headsets to communicate with their own and other US Navy vessels. The system worked reasonably well, even during the large-scale sea and air battles of World War II.

With the advent of high-speed jet fighters, everything changed. When the Navy simulated a Soviet air attack on the US fleet, the results were devastating. They realized that manual plotting on Plexiglas would no longer do. A defense management system that could track faster than humans was needed.

Enter a technology-savvy lieutenant commander at the Navy Electronics Laboratory (NEL) in San Diego, Irvin McNally. He knew about a digital defense management system that IBM had developed for the Air Force, the SAGE project, and he wanted the Navy to pursue something similar. In his mind, every ship should be equipped with a computer that could automatically read radar signals; simultaneously track air, ship, and submarine targets; and automatically compute and rank threats. And every computer should be connected directly, via radio, to all other ships in the battle.

This all sounded good except for one detail: the Air Force's SAGE computer took up twenty-two thousand square feet and weighed 250 tons, and McNally wanted his shipboard computers to be the size of a refrigerator.

What to do?

McNally knew what he was talking about. As a radio engineer, he was aware that the transistor was about to revolutionize the world of digital computers, in size and reliability. The Navy adopted his proposal, and, in 1955, the NTDS project was born. Involving contractors from all over the country, it resulted in Navy vessels being equipped with computers, radar systems, modem transmitters, and peripherals. As computers became smaller, airplanes and even rockets were outfitted in a similar way.

The main contractor selected to design and build computers for Navy vessels was UNIVAC, and the UNIVAC engineer tasked with doing the logic design for the computer at the heart of NTDS was a brilliant technology pioneer whose last name has become synonymous with the word *supercomputer*: Seymour Cray. He stuck with UNIVAC just long enough to design a prototype computer.

When Cray left to join Control Data Corporation, Hy Osofsky was put in charge of the logic redesign. "I was the only one there with any experience who was able to do the design work," Hy later told me about the assignment.

He was being modest. An alum of the Polytechnic Institute in Brooklyn, Hy has degrees in applied mathematics and electronics, and in my view, he and the other people on his team were digital geniuses. Two of them, Finley McLeod and Bob Burkeholder, eventually left UNIVAC together with him to start Atron.

The teams working on the NTDS project included many other specialists from all fields of engineering. Mechanical engineers like me were responsible for the "packaging." We designed, built, and tested the computer cabinet, chassis, printed circuit assemblies, and cables to prove that the machines wouldn't corrode in salt-heavy air or be adversely affected by mechanical shock, vibration, and variations in temperature and humidity. If a blast from a big gun rattled the battleship, the computer needed to stay put. If the water pressure onboard a ship or submarine spiked, the water-chilled coils in the cooling system still had to function.

In 1963, when the Navy deployed a new surveillance and antisubmarine aircraft, the P-3C Orion, they asked UNIVAC to build an airborne computer connecting the P-3C plane with NTDS units on ships. This was a project with which I became heavily involved, first as mechanical design supervisor, then as engineering manager, and finally as manufacturing manager for the new computer.

Because of the space limitations, airborne computers presented a whole new challenge. A typical P-3C flight crew had three pilots, two communication officers, two engineers, three radar and acoustic sensor operators, and one technician. Our solution was to take the design of the shipboard computer and fit it onto a smaller and lighter footprint for airborne use that eventually became known as the CP-901 computer, a thirty-bit machine that used silicon microcircuits. Production deliveries for this breakthrough technology began in 1967.

Consisting of a series of conduction-cooled units that included a central processor, memory, power supply, cables, a control console, and more, the CP-901 had a volume of only 7.4 cubic feet and weighed 306 pounds.

Each individual unit had to be pluggable for easy maintenance and exchange. After all, military electronics must be reliable under very stressful conditions, and no one wants to go into combat with equipment that fails. If a part does break down, the entire system must be operational again in a very short time. This meant that a spare unit had to be onboard in case one of the CP-901 chassis failed. A crew member could then quickly fix the problem.

AS I MOVED from mechanical design supervisor to engineering manager and manufacturing manager, two UNIVAC people became especially important for me. Juel Peterson was my design draftsman. Tasked with developing the ideas that I developed as a mechanical design engineer, he was the one who did the detailed drawings to learn if our ideas might work.

Arnie Hendrickson, who was our division director, was the other. A few levels above me, he was a gifted, well-liked manager. He became my mentor on the CP-901 project.

Juel's introduction to my team was bumpy, but only because I made it so. An administrator by the name of Dale Willie said to me one day, "John, you wanted a design draftsman. I found you one. His name is Juel Peterson."

"Do I get to interview him?"

"No. His table is already set up. He's over there."

A little put out that Dale would choose my designer without consulting me, I picked up some prints that needed modifying and introduced myself to Juel. "Why don't you take the day and look at these, and we'll visit again tomorrow," I suggested.

The next day, I realized that Juel was completely familiar with the prints. "You really studied these," I said.

"John, I was the checker."

My failure to see who had signed as checker of the drawings that I had to sign as engineer made me feel bad. But Juel didn't hold it against me, and we made for a great tandem.

Together with a couple of other guys on our team, we sometimes did additional creative work at Gannon's nearby. We'd go there, put down $1.05, which was good for three Grain Belt beers, and write our ideas on napkins so we wouldn't forget. We were in their piano bar, with the TV on, the night after

President John F. Kennedy was shot, and watched with sadness as his casket was brought back. How could this happen?

Back in the 1960s, alcohol and work weren't necessarily seen as conflicting. While the telephone company that my neighbor Don Lindquist worked for had a zero-tolerance policy, UNIVAC engineers could go out to lunch and have a beer or two.

I will admit, however, that our afterwork sessions occasionally interfered with my family life. Our son, Mike, would complain about my being home later than other fathers. By the time we sat down for dinner, his friends were done eating and out playing again. My defense toward Pat was always, "This isn't social time. We're being especially creative."

All three of our children were born during my time at UNIVAC. When our first daughter, Lisa, arrived one year after Mike, I made a bad judgment call. She was induced and came midday. While I was at the hospital for the delivery, I left soon after, with Pat's consent, and returned to the office to work.

Later that day, after handing out cigars at Gannon's, I told some colleagues, "You should come up and see the new baby."

I should have known better. Pat didn't necessarily like surprises and had no appreciation for informality. Having been in labor only a few hours earlier, she was gracious enough when the guys were in her room. But after they had left, she said, "I just had a baby. You shouldn't be bringing your buddies in here to see me in this situation."

I STAYED WITH UNIVAC for just over a decade—long enough to make many good friends. Among them was a man who shared my last name, Ray Miller. He and his two brothers would often include me in their bowling games and have a lot of fun with me. Being clueless about some of their rules, it seemed that I got stuck paying for all the beer frames. Of course, I was always telling people, "No, I'm not another brother of Ray's."

My first thought to leave UNIVAC arose one summer, when the owner of a connector company in St. Paul pushed me to do sales for him. My boss was on vacation, but I turned in my letter of resignation anyway.

A few events made me rethink my decision. I saw the forlorn look on the face of Juel and two other men in our cubicle, Larry Lesko and Don Fodness. Plus, Ed Kulczycki, a manager in the same area, pulled me aside with advice. "John, your prospects here at UNIVAC are pretty good, and I know the owner of the connector company. You should reconsider."

The Atron team in December 1968: Finley McLeod, Joe Stoutenburgh, Hy Osofsky, Juel Peterson, Dennis Stanga, and Bob Burkeholder (from left to right).

By 1968, when Finley McLeod took me out to lunch one day and asked whether I wanted to join Atron as a managing engineer with equity, my work situation had changed. UNIVAC had gone through a restructuring where parts of Arnie's division were eliminated, and the CP-901 manufacturing department that I managed was now reporting to guys whose technological competence didn't impress me. Maybe I was just cocky, but, at the same time, I had great respect for the talent of Finley, Hy Osofsky, and the other electrical engineers behind Atron. They knew me, and I knew them, and they needed a mechanical engineer to start the design and build their computers. I didn't even have to think twice. As for Juel—he went right with me.

7.

Seeing an Opportunity

ATRON WAS FOUNDED following an idea of a former chief engineer at UNIVAC, Dick Karpen, who was now an executive at MDS in Herkimer, New York. MDS' initial success was based on the development of a punch-card alternative called Keyboard to Magnetic Tape, but they also produced off-line printers and were looking to build a small computer that could drive the printer in place of the mainframe machine.

When Karpen suggested to some of his former UNIVAC colleagues that they should start a company of their own to develop such a computer with MDS as their first customer, Hy, Finley, Bob Burkeholder, Bob Bergman, and some of their UNIVAC colleagues on the business side, like Robert Gountanis and Dennis Stanga, accepted the offer. Hy, who was the first of the team to leave UNIVAC, came up with the name for the new business: "A" for number one, and "tron" for electronic. Atron was born.

I joined soon afterward, as one of nine or ten people with equity, thereby trading my desk at UNIVAC for a corner in a motel room, first in a Holiday Inn and later in a Howard Johnson. To me, this didn't matter. What I cared about was feeling comfortable with my colleagues and that my weekly paycheck kept coming. Given our family lifestyle, this was important. I also felt excited about our long-term goal of being competitive with our own product line of data-entry stations.

Unfortunately, it never came true. Atron struggled to win new customers, and with MDS consistently providing at least 90 percent of our business, the two companies began merger talks soon after we started the Belcourt plant.

I learned of the negotiations during an early-morning shareholder meeting at the legendary Thunderbird Motel in Bloomington, a suburb of Minneapolis, where we were informed that MDS would pull in the manufacturing of products designed on their dime if Atron didn't merge with them. I didn't like the idea. It seemed we were letting down the public that had invested in our stock after our IPO. I also felt bad for the people like Juel that I had brought with me from UNIVAC and for everyone working on the reservation. But I was in the minority.

A vote on the proposed merger went through almost unanimously. By 1974, the two entities had merged, and the management on the East Coast decided to close the Twin Cities location. Juel, at this point, joined Data Card Corporation.

WHEN MDS CLOSED Atron's offices in St. Paul, it was clear to me that they would also shut down the Belcourt facility once they no longer needed core memory; unlike me, the MDS people on the East Coast had no North Dakota affiliation and no experience operating on a reservation. And they were unlikely to feel a commitment toward the workers on the reservation or to people like Bob Wilmot, the NDSU alum who had moved to the area to manage the plant.

Fortunately for us, core died slowly. It was driven from the market gradually between 1973 and 1977, and, in 1974, the memory microcircuits were not yet available. This meant that the plant at Belcourt was still vital to MDS' operations.

I had not considered starting my own business. My goal was to do my best in role I had, and with that came opportunities.

But here I saw an opening. Since MDS knew nothing about the production of core memory and was unlikely to invest in a dying technology, they needed a supplier to manufacture it for them.

In August 1974, I approached the head of manufacturing at MDS Atron with a plan. "How are you going to get your core memory?" I said.

"Well, John, we'll just keep you on the payroll in St. Paul, and then you can manage the plant at Belcourt and the people working from home."

"No," I said. "I will set up a separate company and build and repair core memory for you under contract."

Part B:

The Bootstrap Approach

8.

Where There's a Need, There's a Way

OF ALL THE YEARS I could have picked to start my own company, 1974 was one of the worst. America was in the midst of an economic recession induced by rising oil prices. The inflation rate that year reached 11 percent, and from August to December the unemployment rate jumped from 5.5 percent to 7.2 percent. Of course, it didn't make things better that I should choose to create a contract manufacturing and service business for high-tech electronics with a single product that was becoming obsolete: core memory.

But as with Atron six years earlier, I now felt confident as founder of Turtle Mountain Corporation (TMC).

I had been an engineer in the technology sector for more than one and a half decades. Having spent ten of those years with a military supplier and pioneer in the industry, UNIVAC, I had been on the cutting edge of technology and knew to focus on customer needs and quality.

Add to this that the Belcourt plant had already proven itself as a manufacturer of high-quality core memory at a reasonable cost. I didn't doubt for a second that we would be able to do the same with other electronic products.

Last but not least, Bob wanted to start the company with me as shareholder and stay in charge of the plant at Belcourt.

WHEN I BEGAN negotiating with MDS in New York for our takeover of the plant, neither Bob nor I had cash on hand to buy the operation outright. Since we also didn't have money for inventory or payroll, we had to get creative.

For the production of core memory, we needed various supplies, including printed wiring boards, ferrite cores, and wire/needle assemblies. (Like suture needles used in operating rooms, the needles used for the stringing of core memory don't have an eye. Instead, the wire is already attached.) All these items, together with inventory of core memory at various stages of production, were on hand and owned by MDS.

My plan was that TMC would finish the work in process, use the existing inventory to produce additional core memory, and ship finished product to MDS on a weekly basis—at a negotiated price that included a profit for TMC. Overall, the arrangement addressed TMC's lack of capital and MDS' need for core memory. This would allow us to start operating without having to raise capital. And we would get from MDS equipment available in their facility in the Twin Cities that would prove useful once we started diversifying the plant at Belcourt.

The negotiations with MDS challenged my patience and tested my capacity to persevere. In my first written proposal, addressed to MDS vice president Robert Hingre and dated August 31, 1974, I laid out our market research and shared a list of potential customers that included 3M, UNIVAC, Honeywell, and Steiger Tractor.

Then I wrote, "If Atron is to cease operation, TMC would like very much to build and repair core memory for MDS. Dependent on the production requirement, the TMC build price would likely be very close to the present Atron standard cost. We would expect that MDS would provide all material, pay all shipping costs, pay for maintenance of MDS-owned equipment and pay for installation of equipment not now at Belcourt but needed for memory production (diode welder and freon cleaner)."

Two weeks later, I followed up with details and specified that my proposal was valid until October 1. The date came and went, but finally, in mid-October, MDS manufacturing manager George Sylvester flew up to North Dakota to meet me and assess the plant inventory. Since MDS had no use for any of the items, George gave us a good price.

The letter of agreement that George and I signed on October 17 stated a TMC start-up date of November 18 that MDS soon pushed out to December 2. On November 21, one week before Thanksgiving, even the December date seemed threatened. I sent George a final letter, informing him that the deal would need to be renegotiated if they didn't send me a letter of agreement before Thanksgiving. This worked.

Together, Bob and I founded Turtle Mountain Corporation in St. Paul. We split our total investment of $2,500 (about $15,000 today) with me as majority owner and incorporated on December 7, 1974. On Friday, we were employees of MDS Atron, and the next Monday, we were employees of Turtle Mountain Corporation, an electronics assembly and test business.

Someone asked me recently what it meant to me that TMC was born on Pearl Harbor Day. Well, I was only six years old when Japan bombed Pearl Harbor in 1941 but have not forgotten how my family, with guests visiting from Kenmare, gathered around the radio the following day. The radio sat on a table in the living room, on a doily. President Franklin D. Roosevelt spoke of "a date which will live in infamy."

In hindsight, it seems clear that the events of that day were an awakening for us as a country. People ran to enlist and serve their country. They got to work. In this sense, I was all right with having the date connected to TMC.

But I also knew that we would have to fight to be successful. We had one dying product, core memory, and one customer, MDS. Since they were having trouble paying their bills, the only way we could ship our core memory to them was COD. The Van Lines driver would arrive in New York with the product, and then he'd sit there and wait for a check before handing over the merchandise—because we had payroll for about three dozen employees coming up, and we needed the money.

LIKE MANY OTHER bootstrap entrepreneurs, I initially ran my business from the basement of our home that Pat and I had just bought for our family of five. Located in Shoreview, a family-friendly suburb ten miles north of the Twin Cities, the $16,000 property had three bedrooms, a walkout basement, and a double attached garage.

Bob (left) and I were a good team (late 1980s).

Our later office addresses included an Easy Mini Storage place that had a couple of offices for people like us; upstairs offices of a printed circuit fabricator; and finally, a very nice office and lab area in Vadnais Heights, very close to our Shoreview home. The building owner, an electrical contractor, prepared the offices and meeting rooms as we wanted them. It was important to me that we presented an image of a successful organization to our customers and supplier representatives, since both had the potential to give or refer new business opportunities.

In our office at an Easy Mini Storage, with Bob Wilmot (right) and one of our first employees, Wayne Blilie.

Having our office in St. Paul came with a disadvantage: it was far from the plant at Belcourt. The advantage of being in the Twin Cities was their status as a technology hub, or, as one might say, as a Silicon Valley of the time.

It may sound odd today, but St. Paul once teemed with companies and start-ups that developed computers, components, and peripherals, and the nation's most talented young engineers were eager to move there. In the wake of this boom, we, as a contract manufacturer of high-tech electronic products, could only benefit from having local suppliers and a potentially large local customer base that needed us as a full-service manufacturer of their products.

THE TWIN CITIES' RISE to computing fame began with World War II, when information was a key weapon.[2] The British broke the German codes, the Americans broke the Japanese codes, and both events profoundly impacted the outcome of the war. To get the job done, cryptanalysts had to invent their own methods, design and build their own code-breaking machines, guess their enemies' thoughts, and collaborate with each other, all under immense time pressure.

The codebreakers for the US Navy worked out of a girl's' school campus in Washington, DC, the Mount Vernon Seminary. The operation included scientists, linguists, mathematicians, engineers, typists, and clerical staff. With the men off to the battlefields, many of them were women. In 1944, when the Allies broke the German Enigma code, over three thousand women sworn to secrecy were working at Mount Vernon. After the war, all this brainpower scattered. The government lacked a master plan for retaining its code-breaking capability.

AS SOON AS 1946, two small companies emerged from the war effort. One was in Pennsylvania, the other in Minnesota, and both became leaders in the country's nascent computer industry.

In St. Paul, the synergistic meeting of a Navy codebreaker from the Midwest, Bill Norris, and a patriotic entrepreneur from the East Coast, John Parker, led to the creation of Engineering Research Associates (ERA).[3]

Norris, who was Nebraska-born and had a degree in electrical engineering from the University of Nebraska, worked on the family farm during the Great Depression then sold X-ray equipment in Chicago, and eventually joined the Navy in Washington, DC, as a wartime code breaker. After the war, his Navy superiors, obviously fearing the loss of key know-how, encouraged him to start a private company and promised government contracts.

Being a passionate engineer with an entrepreneurial spirit,

the Midwesterner needed little convincing. He could easily envision a future far beyond military applications for the calculating technologies pioneered at Mount Vernon. What he lacked, however, was money and a space for his business.

Norris teamed up with another code breaker, Howard Engstrom, and together they approached the giants of American business for investment. Raytheon, NCR, and American Airlines turned them down, as did major New York investment banks. The problem was that no one could envision a computer, let alone a market for computers.

Enter John Parker.

A Naval Academy graduate and former investment banker from the East Coast, Parker had spent the war years in St. Paul, manufacturing wooden gliders that the Army used to crash-land troops and equipment behind enemy lines, as was the case on D-Day in Normandy. With the end of the war, Parker's business evaporated overnight. The government-owned old factory building at 1902 Minnehaha Avenue stood dormant.

When Parker was introduced to Norris shortly after the war, it was a perfect match. Parker, who liked living in St. Paul, had capital and factory space—it was the same building on Prior and Minnehaha that I would first enter in 1958 for my interview with UNIVAC—but no product. Norris had a product and a potential customer: the Navy.

Due to the top-secret nature of the business, Norris couldn't tell Parker what they would be selling to the Navy, so Parker traveled to Washington, DC, for assurances. There, Fleet Admiral Chester W. Nimitz, the commander in chief of the US Pacific Fleet in World War II, appealed to his patriotism. This was good enough for Parker.

In January 1946, Parker, Norris, Engstrom, and Navy captain Ralph Meader founded ERA. They immediately hired forty of their former code-breaking Navy colleagues, who all moved to St. Paul to work in the old glider factory.

While I can imagine how exciting it must have felt to these talented people to be a part of the new venture in the Midwest, their job was hardly glamorous. The brick building on the corner of Prior and Minnehaha was large, shabby, and drafty, and, in the summer, ERA's employees shared the space with birds.[4] In the winter, the birds left for warmer places, while the engineers, designers, and scientists toiled on, wearing thick coats.

Meanwhile, in Philadelphia, two University of Philadelphia engineers, Presper Eckert and John Mauchly, were also starting a company. Known as the brains behind the world's first electronic computer, the ENIAC (Electronic Numerical Integrator and Computer), the two men were already legends in their field.

The ENIAC project, which the US Army commissioned during World War II, was created with the purpose of calculating artillery-firing tables.[5] What made the resulting computer groundbreaking was the engineering. As with previous machines, programming the ENIAC still meant manipulating cables and flipping switches. It was a complex process that could keep the initial team of six primary programmers—they were all women—busy for days. But once that work was done, the ENIAC showed its superiority. Different from any previous calculator, it could operate without mechanical switching, relying on electrical circuitry and relays instead. This made it many times faster than any predecessor. Being enormous in size, the world's first computers took a long time to develop and build and cost incredible sums of money.

Eckert and Mauchly, following their success with the ENIAC, started Eckert–Mauchly Computer Corporation with funding from family and friends and from a local businessman in Philadelphia, Henry Straus.[6]

In 1951, the two engineers announced a breakthrough. They had developed the first commercially available digital mainframe computer for business application, the UNIVAC I, which stands for Universal Automatic Computer. Weighing sixteen thousand pounds, it used five thousand vacuum tubes and could make about one thousand calculations per second.

By then, investor Straus had died in a plane crash, which forced the two company founders, who were much better engineers than fundraisers, to sell their business. It was now owned by Remington Rand, a maker of office equipment in Norwalk, Connecticut.

Bill Norris fared similarly to Eckert and Mauchly. By 1951, when his company, ERA, announced its first commercially available computer, the 1101, he was also running out of money. Here, too, Remington Rand stepped in, but just a few years later, even they needed more capital to defend their lead against a very determined IBM. They found a well-funded partner with experience in digital equipment, Sperry Corporation.

After the merger, Sperry Rand made a business decision to consolidate its St. Paul, Philadelphia, and Norwalk computing capabilities into a single division that it called UNIVAC. In October 1955, it appointed Norris to be the division's first general manager.

AS A NORTH DAKOTAN, I am probably biased. But I believe that the story of St. Paul's rise to computer fame also speaks to a cultural difference between two regions, the East Coast and the Midwest with its more laid-back style.

Take the story of Hy Osofsky, who is from New York and started his career at Westinghouse in Baltimore, Maryland, where he worked on a ground-controlled missile-defense system that Boeing was developing for the Air Force. When Westinghouse needed to buy a computer for the project, they tasked him with the purchase. The only place to go was ERA in the Twin Cities.

"I went to St. Paul and loved it right away," Hy told me. "It was small, there wasn't much traffic, and the people were friendly." He remembers the work environment at Westinghouse as "regimented" and backward. "I had to sign in if I was late," he told me. In 1955, he left Baltimore for St. Paul and joined UNI-VAC. "The people there were doing new things," he said, "and there was much more excitement."

WHEN I JOINED UNIVAC, three years after Hy, the excitement was still there, though Bill Norris had left to start another Minnesota tech company that would become legendary, Control Data Corporation (CDC), and had taken with him an entire team of engineers.

Among them was the first NTDS logic designer, the already-mentioned Seymour Cray, who came from Chippewa Falls, Wisconsin. Drafted into World War II as a radio operator, Cray helped break Japanese naval codes before earning degrees in engineering and mathematics from the University of Minnesota. He made Control Data an instant player in the computer industry. Their second computer model, the CDC 6600, ran ten times faster than any other system on the market.

In 1972, two years before I started TMC, Bill Norris gave Cray $300,000 to start his own company in Minneapolis, Cray Research.[7] Computers designed and produced by Cray, who died in a car accident in 1996, remained the fastest in the world throughout the 1970s and 1980s.

Norris and Cray's start-ups weren't the only spinoffs that turned the Twin Cities into tech central. Dozens of others, including Atron, grew out of UNIVAC and Control Data, which both employed thousands of people. Even IBM moved in. Its IBM Rochester facility eventually grew to 3.1 million square feet and became known for the midrange AS/400 computer series that was launched in 1985 and is still made and sold today as IBM i.

AS WITH SILICON VALLEY, one reason for the proliferation of technology companies in Minneapolis and St. Paul was a culture of investing. Spin-offs like Control Data offered stock options to their initial employees and sold shares to friends and former colleagues at one dollar a piece. A typical engineer at UNIVAC might have had an investment in multiple small tech companies, had his broker's number posted next to his phone, and met regularly with other engineers in organized investment clubs.[8]

Lacking excess cash for investing, I was atypical at UNIVAC and didn't own stock. But I remember how Ray Miller used to tell us about his Control Data shares and how another colleague talked about selling half of his investment to buy a new Buick. As time went on and the value of Control Data shares kept rising, people began to wonder how much that Buick really cost.

With ever more stock-owning engineers in the Twin Cities doing well thanks to the spectacular growth of some start-ups, many used their funds to strike out on their own. I imagine that most of these fledgling entrepreneurs went into their new ventures with the same enthusiasm that I brought to Atron after leaving UNIVAC—and many must have felt disappointed when they didn't make it.

In the early days of Atron, I told friends, "I have all these Atron shares. When the company takes off, I'll charter a plane, and we'll fly to Jamaica." In the end, I could have just about taken them to Jamestown, North Dakota—on a bus.

In hindsight, I believe that several factors contributed to Atron's failure. The company grew rapidly in the beginning, adding new people at a fast pace. But like many other tech start-ups in the Twin Cities, we lacked a strong marketing and sales department.

THERE'S A STORY about a bright young man from North Dakota, Doug Burgum, who, in 1983, joined a start-up in Fargo called Great Plains Accounting. Their product was a hard-disk accounting series that ran on Microsoft DOS.

To promote the fledgling business, Doug rented space at Comdex, a national computer trade show that was in Atlanta that spring. He gave his booth a theme, "Rope a Winner," outfitted it with roping steers, bales of hay, and a few feet of split-rail fence, and wore jeans, cowboy boots, and a hat as he chatted up visitors.

The attention-grab worked.

People stopped for roping, buttons, and prizes, and a young twenty-four-hour cable news channel, CNN, reported live from the show with Doug's booth in the background and the Great Plains name getting its first national TV publicity.

Later that year, he reprised the production at Las Vegas Fall Comdex, where thousands of vendors presented in booths of all sizes. On the second day, the trade-show special newspaper that was distributed to every Vegas hotel room featured a top-half, center-of-page photo of a rancher from North Dakota, John Hanson, throwing a loop in the Great Plains booth.

Under Doug's leadership, the company grew, went public in the late 1990s, and was acquired by Microsoft in 2001 for $1.1 billion. Now, there's a big contingent of Microsoft in Fargo—and Doug is the governor of North Dakota.

By comparison, Atron seemed lame. Bob Bergman once showed me something he had created.

"It's a computer with a microcircuit, all on one board the size of a plate," he said.

As a mechanical engineer responsible for manufacturing, I will admit that seeing the future of computer evolution was a bit out of my league, but I thought that Bob's invention, which didn't go to market, had potential.

Hy remembers realizing early on that Atron wouldn't make it. "There were many talented engineers at Atron, but there was no business plan," he said. "We were tied to MDS, didn't have a strategy for finding our market, and flailed around."

This is what venture capitalists in Silicon Valley would now call finding your product-market fit.

After the merger with MDS, which was a stock swap with no cash involved, a legend on the original Atron stock certificate prohibiting the sale of shares within the first five years of going public disappeared, and I was free to turn my MDS stock into cash at any time.

For a while, Pat and I entertained ideas of owning a Dairy Queen franchise, a chain for which she had worked as a student at NDSU. The perfect spot, so we thought, was not far from our house. It was on the highway and right by a junior high school. When we proposed the location to Dairy Queen International, they said, "That's all well and good, Mr. Miller, but we alone pick where our stores go."

Months later, Dairy Queen called to say that they agreed with the location. They suggested that we proceed with the project, but Pat and I dallied on the decision.

Sometime later, I saw a hole being dug right where we had planned to put our Dairy Queen. I went over to my neighbor, who's a developer. "Bob, do you know what's going on over there?"

"Sure," he said. "They're putting in a Dairy Queen."

Lesson learned: don't dally.

9.

Failure Is Not an Option

ANYONE GOING INTO BUSINESS the way I did after the closing of Atron will find their life fundamentally changed. As a bootstrap entrepreneur starting a service company like TMC, I was, at least for the time being, in the right place. The Twin Cities' status as a preeminent tech hub lasted until the mid-1970s, and many of the engineers striking out with start-ups were designers with little experience in the manufacturing of electronic products. For them, contracting for their production was a good, cost-saving option.

But faced with a deadline because our only product was a dying technology, we had to book new production. For me, the task of finding new customers and diversifying became all-consuming. It never went away.

I remember making a sales call one day to an engineer at 3M. As we were ending our meeting, he said to me, "I really admire what you're doing, John. How do you handle it?"

It's possible that his question came from a desire to also start a business. But I walked away, thinking, *He admires what I'm doing? Well, I admire the job he has. He's getting a regular paycheck.*

Struggling to stay in business, I sometimes had these thoughts: *My God, what if we run out of money? What are we going to do before we get these customers?*

Did I ever despair or think of giving up? No. Too much depended on our success.

Walking around the empty plant at night, I would see our employees' workstations and think of these people's reliance on me, Bob, and our team to maintain an opportunity—a job—for them.

Add to this that Pat and I were never big savers. When I was at UNIVAC, there was a small pension plan, and having bought our first home in 1960, we had some equity when I started TMC. But given our age and our family situation, with three children in school, I knew this much: Other than bankruptcy, or the potential return to UNIVAC, as others had done, both options that I did not think about, there was no road back for us. And if we were ever going to retire, failure was not an option.

MONEY MANAGEMENT was a problem for Pat and me. Pat claimed that she had learned as a home economics student that the best way to keep your husband hustling is to spend more money than he makes. Having come from different environments, we had different spending habits. In my family, without anyone mentioning it, we all knew that funds were limited. My folks never bought anything until they had saved the money to pay for it. I doubt that they ever had a loan or a credit card. In Pat's family, the frequent moves and housing changes made it difficult to accumulate savings.

When we were in Fort Sill, Pat and I almost fell into a debt trap ourselves. In the Army, there was always the option to get a payday loan. But I became tired of doing that—not to mention that it wasn't sustainable in the long term.

After I joined UNIVAC, we had $108 a week, which was better but still not much, considering that Pat was a student at the university. Unfortunately, my department was known all around for being stingy. The first time my gross salary increased, the difference was so minor that I thought I had completed my social security contribution.

At lunch, I mentioned it to one of my engineering friends, who said, "Did your gross change?"

I went back to the office and found Earl.

"I got $2.18 more in my check. That wasn't my raise, was it?"

"Yes, John, and we sure feel bad about that. But we're taking your case up to the chief engineer, and it will get fixed."

Another time, I went over to Plant 5, where some NDSU classmates were sitting around and reading as they waited for their next contract.

Over in Plant 2, we were swamped. I asked a couple of them, "Why don't you transfer over and help us out?"

"Are you crazy?" they said. "We heard about the low pay."

OUR FINANCIAL SITUATION as a family improved after Pat received her degree and found a part-time teaching job that took her to downtown St. Paul, although her work also caused some trouble: she was accumulating parking tickets.

The fine was never much, maybe two or three dollars apiece, but the notices kept piling up before we mailed them in.

One day, Pat called me from our apartment.

"The sheriff is here. He has a warrant for your arrest for non-payment of traffic tickets."

I went down to City Hall. "I mailed the payments," I told the clerk. "I don't think I should be paying twenty-five dollars in addition to what I have already paid."

"You did, but there are late fees. Do you want to see a judge and appeal this?"

I did.

The traffic court room upstairs was full, which gave me time to think about a brief speech. Finally, my case was called: "The City of St. Paul and the County of Ramsey versus John Miller."

I stepped up to the bench—and choked up. The feeling of insecurity must have gotten to me. Next thing I knew, a policeman standing beside me was rapping me on the knuckles and admonishing me. "Keep your hand out of your pocket when you're in front of a judge."

"Tell me your story," the judge said.

"Well, Your Honor, I'm supposed to pay twenty-five dollars because of nonpayment of traffic tickets. But I paid them."

"You paid them?"

"I paid them, but some arrived late."

"Is there anyone who can verify this?"

"I was downstairs, and the clerk confirmed what I'm telling you."

The judge ordered me to sit down, sent for the clerk, and swore her in.

"Mr. Miller is telling you the truth," she said.

I got by with a late fee of three dollars, and not long after my court appearance, the tickets stopped coming. Pat had switched to teaching full-time and was now in a different location. It had a parking lot.

PAT'S ENTRY into the teaching profession, in 1960, came from a longing to own a home. When I started at UNIVAC, the mechanical engineer in the desk next to me, Les Nesler, was building a house in a new subdivision that Rehbein-Husnick contractors were developing. Since this was the company's second project in the Shoreview area, a house at the original site functioned as the model home and sales office.

After checking on the progress of his house a few times with Les, I decided to visit again with Pat and baby Mike on a Sunday afternoon. Pat liked what she saw, and so we drove from there straight to Rehbein-Husnick's project office, where Elmo Lillehaugen dove into a sales pitch that led to us heading right back to the development with Elmo. "Pick your lot," he said.

With the lot chosen and all options determined—we wanted a walkout basement and a double attached garage—the only thing between us and homeownership was the funding. But Pat's mind was set. "I'll teach if we buy," she said. Elmo prepared the paperwork, I gave him two fifty-cent pieces that I found in my pocket as down payment on the contract, and we signed.

As for the $1,100 down payment on the property, Rehbein-Husnick offered us a $600 discount if we did the painting and staining ourselves. That sounded good. By this time, UNIVAC had raised my weekly salary to $125 (about $1,200 today), which would equal our monthly payment on the house for principal, interest, taxes, and insurance combined. But driving away from the development on that Sunday afternoon, I thought, *What have we done? Where will we scrape up the remaining $500 and the money for paint supplies?*

ONE AND A HALF DECADES LATER, during my first few years as an entrepreneur, pursuing potential customers was an all-day commitment. Unless I could convince one to go see a Vikings game or shoot a round of golf, I was on the phone attempting to develop a relationship. All other work had to wait until nighttime or the weekend.

Every other week, I sat down with a sack of bills and wrote as many checks as I could. Of course, the sack always filled up with new bills.

One day, Pat stepped into my office in the basement. "You wanted to start a business," she said, "so we must make it go. Is there anything I can do?"

"Well, how about the family finances?"

Pat was okay with that and went upstairs, sack in hand. The next day, she came back. "I got it all done, but there's not enough money."

"No shit!"

Pat took that sack and threw it right at me. I picked it up and threw it right back at her.

After that, she kept track of where the money was going. Her new role as the family treasurer affected her and our spending—and I now had a difficult time getting money out of her. This, of course, was Pat's nature. She had a task, and she was going to do it right. Why hadn't I given her that job years earlier?

10.

Building a Team

MILLIONS OF ARTICLES must have been written on which type of personality is best suited for entrepreneurship. But I believe that putting together the right team is just as important to the long-term success of a company. I learned as an employee at UNIVAC, and then at Atron, the importance of unity, trust, dedication, and competence at the leadership level and within a team. During my time at UNIVAC, I was happiest when working with my design draftsman, Juel Peterson, and my mentor, Arnie Hendrickson. Atron didn't work out perfectly. But seeing what went wrong there was instructive in its own way. I brought both experiences with me to TMC.

The people who made the biggest difference at TMC were without doubt Pat and my partner, Bob. Pat, who had given up teaching in 1966 before the birth of our youngest child, Kristi, trusted me with the business. More than that, she supported it in an active way. In the beginning, she continued to supervise core-memory stringers who worked from home in places around Minnesota and Wisconsin, a job she had started while I was still at Atron.

Having previously done this work for Control Data or Fabritech, the at-home core-memory stringers were experienced and, in some cases, very fast. We had to limit the number of boards issued to them per week so that their work time wouldn't exceed forty hours and require overtime pay.

Pat, who later became indispensable to TMC as treasurer, really enjoyed working with the women in the at-home program and getting to know them. When she met with them to give them a check for previous work, she would also present them with a quality report. Apparently, the women loved comparing the reports among one another, much like schoolchildren do at the end of a school year. For them, it was a competition. I bet the top performers were more eager to share their reports, while others remained quiet but determined to do better on their next core memories.

In addition to Pat and Bob, I had a group of professionals and advisers at my side that every business may eventually need. It included our CPA, a banker, an attorney, and very engaged and forthright board members.

Our initial attorney, Carl Swenson, was someone Pat and I knew from church. He helped with the incorporation of TMC, advised us during the start-up phase—and amused us with his nice sense of humor.

I remember Pat needing reassurance when we finally had to go to the bank for money and personally guarantee the loan. "What happens if we don't pay it back?" she asked Carl.

"I think you'll get to keep your bra," he said.

Pat laughed about this. She was still concerned, but she signed.

Our CPA was Willard "Bill" Patty, who held a position as managing partner of a small accounting firm, Taylor, McCaskill & Co, that later merged with Ernst and Young. Bill also connected us with a great young attorney, Mike McEllistrem, who was quick to get to the root of problems and find a solution.

Pat and I first met Bill and his wife, Missy, through friends in the church choir. After I mentioned to him that we needed an accountant, Bill said, "Why don't you do it yourself, and we'll just give you directions and help you?"

That's exactly what happened. Pat started doing the books, and one of the guys in Bill's office, Frank Mukai, made sure we did our payroll and created the necessary reports. Bill and Frank loved the fact that Pat would not stop until the books balanced down to the penny, no matter what time of night it might be.

Finally, our board members proved invaluable. Bill Patty joined the TMC board of directors after his retirement and helped us immeasurably with the financial management of the company. In addition to him, we had Roger Durkee and Randy Erickson. Roger was a retired engineer from Honeywell. Randy and I met in the choir. Among other things, the two men helped prepare a very successful incentive bonus pay plan for our factory management team.

Randy's strength was in the improvement of functioning organizations. A former 3M technical director and NDSU alum like me, but with a PhD in chemistry, he loved traveling to North Dakota, visiting with the staff, and observing operations. He talked to people at the plant, and because of his outside position some of them were more open with him than they were with me. If his opinion about personnel or operations differed from mine, we'd discuss it. His directness helped me evaluate my own position.

IN THE CASE OF TMC, one other person was indispensable: Frank X. Morin. Frank was born on the reservation, attended NDSU in the late 1930s, experienced combat as a soldier in World War II, and had a degree from South Dakota State University. His talent was bringing different people and interest groups together.

What impressed me most about Frank, who later moved to Dunseith and became the mayor there, was his calming presence. It reminded me of other members of the Greatest Generation, like Mel Koenig in Underwood and Donald Vizanko, a colleague at UNIVAC. Don had been stationed in the

Philippines during World War II as a Navy radio specialist and radar officer, which is always a dangerous position. He had the ability to correct or challenge you in a way that would put a smile on your face and make you feel good. With both him and Frank, it was my impression that the experience of war affected the way they managed people. Or maybe it was even bigger: that their perspective and priorities changed.

Frank X. Morin was instrumental to TMC's success.

In 1971, when I was first exploring the possibility of a Turtle Mountain plant, Frank must have been in his midfifties, and the Bureau of Indian Affairs (BIA), which operates within the Department of the Interior, had just named him superintendent of their Turtle Mountain Agency. He was obviously put there to ease tension on the reservation in the context of nationwide protests that had been making headlines.

The Chippewa on the reservation had a lot of respect for Frank, as they generally do for their elders. And we, at TMC, eventually felt so grateful for his contributions that we named one of our conference rooms in his honor. The only other meeting room with a designation was the Pat Miller Conference Room.

Frank told me more than once that he didn't know what his tribe would have done without the plant that Atron started and TMC took over. But he had it backward; without him, we might not have created the Belcourt plant and there might never have been a Turtle Mountain Corporation.

THE EARLY 1970s were a turbulent, militant time in the relationship between Native Americans and the government. In 1968, an urban grassroots group, the American Indian Movement (AIM), had formed in Minneapolis. Their goals included economic independence for indigenous people, autonomy over tribal areas, and the restoration of lands. In 1969 and 1970, AIM made international headlines with a nineteen-month occupation of Alcatraz.

I have sometimes wondered whether the plant at Belcourt would have been possible if I had proposed moving Atron's core-memory production there only one or two years later, when tension between the government and the tribes reached an apex.

Toward the end of 1972, AIM organized a cross-country caravan called the "Trail of Broken Treaties." Seven hundred activists from two hundred tribes and twenty-five states convened in St. Paul and marched on Washington, DC, hoping to meet with President Nixon. When this didn't happen, some five hundred AIM activists occupied the Department of Interior headquarters and destroyed records and property in protest. One of their leaders, Vernon Bellecourt, famously said, "We have now declared war on the United States of America—seek your stations."[9]

The following year, AIM organized an armed protest at Wounded Knee that led to a standoff between activists on one side and the FBI, US Marshals, and the National Guard on the other. Gunfire occurred on both sides, leaving one US Marshal seriously wounded and two Native Americans killed. Under these circumstances, would Atron's leadership still have consented to us creating a plant?

GIVEN THE POLITICAL SITUATION, the idea that one might create a manufacturing facility on a reservation must have seemed outlandish to many people. But times were economically tough in 1971. As a country, we were in a crisis dubbed the Great Inflation. Government expenses were running high because of the Vietnam War and foreign aid, and Europe and Japan competed with us for exports. The US dollar had been stuck in a spiral of devaluation for more than five years, and the unemployment numbers kept rising.

Atron, which had about $2 million in the bank after going public, was not exactly cash-strapped. But in my role as head of manufacturing, I was always trying to control expenses, and one of our biggest cost items was the labor for the production of core memory.

What made the plan realistic was the tribal leadership's willingness to support it.

In my first meeting with Jim, the tribal chairman, I learned that he liked the idea of a Turtle Mountain factory, probably because I came with a recommendation from Louis Amyotte, my Chippewa colleague at Atron.

Two other people to whom I was introduced were also enthusiastic. One of them was Cornelius "Corny" Grant, a tribal member who worked for the EDA. He watched for funding opportunities. The other was Gary Heitman, who was employed by the BIA. He worked hard to prepare for our use the building that the Chippewa were offering us at no charge. At the time of my initial visit, it functioned as a commodity disbursement center and was, therefore, full of freezers. But the tribe was willing to have it painted and later get it weatherized. In the winter, after all, the area is one of the coldest in the contiguous US.

I was just a young engineer back then. But as I left the reservation and took one more look at the building and an artesian well next to it where people were filling up their water tanks, I thought, *I think these guys are all right. I like them, and they're offering us a facility at no charge.* All we had to do was get the equipment and job opportunities up there.

Upon my return from North Dakota to Atron in St. Paul, I first approached my boss, "Mac" McLeod, with the suggestion. A gifted engineer from Wyoming and company director, he was immediately receptive to the idea. He knew Louis Amyotte and thought that supporting the tribe in this way was the right thing to do.

President Joe Stoutenburgh was not nearly as enthusiastic when Mac and I went to see him. Reservations were probably an unfamiliar territory for him; in fact, I'm not sure that he even had much experience with North Dakota. When he finally consented to the plan, his words were "All right, John. You can do this. Just don't get us in trouble."

Given the political tension at the time, Joe may not have agreed to us creating the factory at Belcourt if it hadn't been for Frank. Acting as a liaison between the Chippewa and us, he supported the idea from the start, and his personality and status with the tribe allowed me to assure Joe that there would not be any unrest on the reservation.

Having convinced Joe, I set out to find someone who would be able to manage the plant on the reservation. When none of my engineers at Atron showed an interest in moving to North Dakota, I contacted one of my former NDSU professors, Thomas Sakshaug, to see if he had graduating seniors to recommend. "I need an engineer to come down to St. Paul for training and then go back to North Dakota to set up a manufacturing facility," I said. Since there weren't a lot of engineering opportunities at that point, Tom posted a help-wanted ad on the bulletin board. Dave Siebel ripped it off, showed it to his roommate, Bob Wilmot, and they sent in two applications and came to see me. I hired them both.

BOB, WHOM I SENT to North Dakota, was a good candidate to get the facility in Belcourt going and in charge from day one. An intelligent and caring self-starter, he learned fast and on the job, thereby making up for his lack of experience. It probably also helped that he was a devout Roman Catholic.

Belcourt was named after a French-Canadian Roman Catholic priest, Georges-Antoine Belcourt. A passionate advocate for the American Indian communities, he petitioned the governments in Canada and the US on their behalf, attempting to limit the trade of alcohol and trying to protect Indian traders from unfair treatment by fur companies.[10] In the 1840s, he was sent by the church to Pembina, 130 miles east of Belcourt, to convert the Ojibwe to Catholicism.

In 1882, Congress designated a small tract of land in Rolette County as a reservation for the Turtle Mountain Band of Chippewa. Its high population density resulted from an apparent error: Congress accounted for two hundred Ojibwe and not for the more than one thousand Métis living among them.[11]

With the establishment of the reservation, the Ojibwe and Métis, who traditionally sustained their families with fishing and hunting, lost much of their livelihood. Economic opportunities only improved in the 1930s, when President Franklin Delano Roosevelt's Works Progress Administration (WPA) brought jobs in road construction to the reservation and women were given training and jobs in sewing, cooking, and canning.

After World War II, federal legislative initiatives sought to improve the economic independence and self-determination of

American Indian people. The Economic Opportunity Act of 1965, the Indian Civil Rights Act of 1968, and the 1975 Indian Self-Determination and Education Assistance Act all aimed at eliminating poverty and increasing the self-sufficiency of American Indian communities. In 1972, one year after we started the plant, the Turtle Mountain Reservation chartered its first school for higher education, Turtle Mountain Community College.

The Roman Catholic tradition on the reservation has remained strong. The parish of St. Ann's at Belcourt, which runs an elementary school, is the largest Catholic parish in North Dakota.[12] The church is located just a few miles from the plant.

AFTER WE MADE the decision to go ahead with the reservation plant, I occasionally wondered how things would work out there—would there be unrest? Would people show up to work?

Fortunately for TMC, tensions between Native American tribes and federal and state governments mostly subsided by the mid-1970s. The Wounded Knee occupation, which lasted seventy-one days, was the last major AIM-organized protest, and our work at Belcourt remained unaffected by the political situation.

One of the only problems we encountered in connection with the plant had everything to do with the actions of one or two employees in St. Paul and little with the Chippewa. It was all about stereotyping.

In the initial training phase in the Twin Cities, which took three months, some of our experienced Minnesota workers taught the Chippewa women to string and solder core-memory boards. This was in the summer, and I was on vacation with my family.

One day, when I called the office to see how things are going, Mac told me about a problem. "The instructors found a couple of bugs on the product," he said. "And my friend at the university who's an entomologist identified them as crabs."

Apparently, this prompted protests from the instructors. "We're not going back into that conference room until you get rid of the crabs," they said.

Next thing, they took all the Chippewa women to a local clinic to check for crabs. Not one of them had a bug.

Now, the students were upset. "We're not going back to training until you get the crabs situation fixed."

What a fiasco! The whole story irked me: somebody had been making assumptions about the Chippewa women.

A TMC employee assembling a core memory board.

AFTER WE GOT the plant going, we created an incentive plan for the workers to encourage quality workmanship and regular attendance. Based on our production experience in St. Paul, we established a standard number of hours to string and solder a memory unit. To link each assembly to its assembler, we assigned a serial number to every board in production. This way, we could tie the product back to a specific worker. If errors were found, or a core cracked and needed to be replaced, it became a chargeable error. At the end of the month, workers with a good work record would get a bonus in their paycheck made up of a half hour's pay for every hour under the standard, minus deductions for quality issues. If the employee was absent during the time of work on her board, there was no bonus paid for that board.

We also had a milestone incentive. If a worker completed one hundred units of core memory, they'd get a small gift; for example, a popcorn popper.

When Atron's accountant learned about these gifts, he said, "What's the value of the popper? Because we must report that as part of their earnings for tax purposes."

I just stood there in disbelief. I could take employees out to lunch and spend much more than it cost me to buy a popper for an assembly worker. And now somebody was suggesting the worker should claim the gift on their W-2?

Craziness!

As it turned out, the average stringing time at our Turtle Mountain plant was 20 percent less than the standard we had been experiencing in St. Paul, and the Belcourt factory was the quietest manufacturing place I ever experienced. Of course, there wasn't a lot of machinery, but more importantly the workers policed themselves. If there was a lot of conversation going on, one of the core-memory stringers would turn around and say, "I want to get a bonus, and you're interrupting my work here."

True to Louis Amyotte's prediction that the women of his tribe would be excellent core-memory stringers because of their experience with bead work, the quality of the goods manufactured on the reservation was excellent. The Chippewa women had a sharp eye for their work and even for faulty manufacturing supplies.

On one of my visits, I was saying hello to the workers in the production area and watching as a young woman picked up a new board and a fresh set of wires to string the cores.

She turned to me. "We have a problem, John. We have faulty needles."

The needle looked fine to me, but defective needles were likely to crack a core, and cracked cores resulted in a pay deduction for the worker and rework expense for the company. "What do you mean?"

"The point of the needle is not in the middle. It's like a chisel."

"Really? Let me get the microscope."

The young woman picked up a bunch of needles, inspected them with her naked eye and sorted them into good ones and bad ones. A look through the microscope confirmed that she was right in every case, and we made sure to replace the faulty needles.

Political concerns about starting a manufacturing plant on an American Indian reservation luckily proved unwarranted. Thanks to Frank, there was no unrest on the reservation after we started operations there. And Bob's leadership and compassion made our workers feel that they were in good hands. If one of them needed money, they knew that they could turn to him for an advance.

Just as importantly, the bottom line confirmed that we had been right about moving our core-memory production from St. Paul to Belcourt. In its first year of operation, the new plant saved Atron money.

What eventually impacted me more than any outside turmoil were differences between various stakeholders and interest groups at Belcourt, and their politics. Jim Henry, the tribal chairman with whom I dealt until 1978, was just as big a supporter of TMC and the plant as Frank. But Jim's successor thought differently, and my perception of the tribal government was that if you're in, you're in, and if you're out, you're really out.

11.

Jobs for Young People

IT WOULD BE EASY for me to claim that economic development was my main goal when I pushed for a manufacturing operation on a Native American reservation. It wasn't. I was, however, happy to support an underserved area of my home state.

Just like the overall US population, the people at Belcourt constituted a broad mix.

In the economically difficult years of the 1970s, I noticed that Chippewa who had previously left for work elsewhere returned to the reservation to be closer to family and have access to commodities. Some of them stayed on welfare. Others wanted to be independent, and both Bob and I enjoyed seeing our employees' perspective and life change as they gained work experience at TMC.

Especially among the young Chippewa, there were many whose talents hadn't been acknowledged. Suddenly, they had work and a paycheck. They were developing new skills like stringing magnetic core memory and soldering. And they were receiving acknowledgment for their good work.

As Frank once said in an NDSU story about TMC, "The young people are key to this thing. They're earning income rather than getting it from the welfare office. They can be proud of it."[13]

With the establishment of the plant, two different worlds met on the reservation. Early on, when Atron was still deliberating our plans for a Belcourt factory, Mac and I visited the reservation together and stopped at the American Legion club.

One of the locals was sitting at the bar. "What do you guys do?" he said.

Mac turned to me. "John, tell him what we do."

"We design and build computers."

The man's eyes widened. "Wow!" he said. "I met a guy who ties his own fishing flies, and I thought that was impressive."

One or two years later, Atron organized a large media event at Belcourt. The governor was there along with other politicians and EDA representatives, and Joe Stoutenburgh was there with his wife. I think it was the Stoutenburgh's first visit to a reservation—and I know that it meant a lot to the workers to have so many high-profile people out there. It made them feel seen.

THE TRANSFORMATION that I saw happen at Belcourt sometimes reminded me of changes in my hometown after 1945. The end of World War II brought a series of construction projects to the area. In Underwood, big earth movers dug trenches for water and sewer lines, making outhouses a thing of the past. And just north of town, the US Army Corps of Engineers started a major project on the Missouri River, construction of the 3.4-miles-long Garrison Dam.

The Big Muddy is usually a relatively calm river. But in a flood year, it can discharge more water than almost any other river; exceptions are the Amazon, the Congo, the Ganges, and the Yangtze.[14] In past centuries, major floods occurred annually, and about once a decade, these floods caused major destruction.

I was still in elementary school when the river devastated the city of Omaha in 1943 and inundated its airport with seven feet of water. The flood prompted urgent proposals to Congress to initiate construction of a series of new dams across the Missouri Basin in Montana, the Dakotas, and Nebraska.

Two competing project plans were developed. One, by the Army Corps of Engineers, focused on navigation and power generation. The other, by the US Bureau of Reclamation, focused on irrigation.[15]

The final proposal, hashed out in Omaha on the behest of President Franklin D. Roosevelt, became known as the Pick-Sloan Plan. Named after its coauthors, Lewis A. Pick of the Corps and William Glenn Sloan of the Reclamation Bureau, the plan included five Missouri river dams. The largest was Garrison Dam, just fourteen miles from Underwood.

After Roosevelt died in 1945, the project was again subject to debate. Farmers wanted irrigation, cities wanted water and power, and others wanted to focus on navigation or flood control. Not surprisingly, those who stood to lose their land and livelihoods, mostly farmers and Native Americans, were altogether opposed.

In the end, it was decided that the dam should generate power and provide water for irrigation and the cities east of the dam as Pick and the Army Corps of Engineers had proposed. Apparently, this choice was made because local and state authorities preferred engineers from the Army Corps over officials from the Department of the Interior, which was seen as a more bureaucratic entity. The explanation sounded right to me.

Most impacted by the Garrison Dam project were the three affiliated tribes of the Fort Berthold Reservation the Mandan, Hidatsa, and Arikara. Construction of the dam resulted in the relocation of 80 percent of their tribal membership, flooding of their towns and many sacred sites, and loss of 95 percent of their agricultural land. The land they received in exchange was mostly arid, but years later, surprisingly and luckily, it became part of the North Dakota oil patch.

In May 1948, the three tribes of the Fort Berthold Reservation formally accepted the US government's offer for reimbursement. At the signing ceremony, held in Washington,

DC, their tribal leader, George Gillette, wept. "We will sign this contract with a heavy heart," he said. "With a few scratches of the pen, we will sell the best part of our reservation. Right now, the future does not look too good for us."[16]

Preparations for the project started even before then.

As early as 1946, we, in Underwood, saw a cluster of boom towns spring up on the roads leading to the dam site. One year later, after another severe flood prompted the immediate release of funds, ground was broken for the excavation of the dam proper.

Built as housing for the thousands of people who would be working on the dam, the new towns overlooked what was then the Missouri River but would soon become Lake Sakakawea, so named after the young Shoshone woman who accompanied Lewis and Clark as an interpreter on their westward expedition.

Teeming with entrepreneurially minded people, some of whom were hustlers looking for quick money, the new towns on the dam bore names like Dakota City, Big Bend, Gateway, American City, and Silver City. At their center was Riverdale, which served as the headquarters for the Army Corps of Engineers project. Government-owned, the town was designed to be family-friendly, with schools, a shopping center, movie theater, restaurant, and even a bowling alley and beer parlor.

For us kids, it was an altogether exciting time.

In a place like Underwood, class sizes are small, and you get to know the people with whom you grow up very well. When I was in high school, if we wanted to see new faces, we had to either leave town or wait for country-school kids to visit Underwood with their families on Saturdays.

With the construction of the dam, this changed. In the summer, between 2,000 and 2,500 people worked on the project. Their children brought new life into town, and job opportunities opened for young people.

I landed my first dam-related job when the owners of an electrical and a sheet metal shop in Underwood, TeRoy Repnow and Russell Shere, won a contract to install furnaces in Riverdale homes. While the two men worked on-site in Riverdale, I stayed behind in their shop making aluminum ductwork parts.

In 1953, the summer before college, I found a job with the Army Corps of Engineers, working on a survey crew that was led by two Underwood World War II veterans, Mel Koenig and Raymond "Famous" Preisinger. I learned much later, from an article in the *Underwood News*, that Mel had been a patrol bomber flight engineer with the US Army Air Corps, flying missions over Germany.[17] Like many other veterans, neither he nor Famous talked much about their experiences.

Working with the survey crew meant being away from home Monday through Friday, with occasional overtime on Saturdays. We measured elevation and took soil samples at various intervals, on land and the riverbed, upstream from the dam site all the way to Williston, 125 miles northwest of Underwood. The Corps apparently was concerned about the amount of sediment the Big Muddy would bring to the reservoir. This was hard work because of the need to have full visibility and access for the surveying process. It often meant cutting away brush and small trees. It also provided ample opportunities for poison ivy, which hit me hard more than once.

Along with a couple of other guys on the crew, I had a lot to learn. But Mel and Famous were good examples of delegating, and we also had a lot of fun. We had a sack lunch, which four of us crew members ate in the crew cabin. A piece of plywood that rested on our knees as we sat facing each other served as our table. Mel, and sometimes Famous, occasionally joined us. As the youngster of the group, I'd watch what they had in their sack, and if there was something that looked good, I'd attempt to steal it. Then trouble would erupt.

One time, I grabbed a cupcake that was sitting there, expecting one of them to say, "Leave that alone." Famous watched my every move but didn't say a word.

As I put the treat up to my mouth, I noticed the smell of caulking compound. I examined the cupcake, sniffed it, looked at the two guys sitting across from me, saw the grins on their faces—and threw the cupcake at Famous.

He was a mess.

Leaning across the plywood board, he peeled the smashed cupcake off his face and rubbed it into mine.

Later that day, my folks showed up for a surprise visit.

"I brought fried chicken for the crew," Mom said before noticing the dried caulk around my eyes and nose. "What's all over your face?"

"We put stakes up for surveying," I said, avoiding the full truth. "I had to paint some of them, and it was windy."

Working with Mel Koenig (right) was a good learning experience.

I worked hard, learned a lot, and had fun during those weeks at the dam. Being strong, young, and on the bottom rung, I was often expected to carry heavy equipment. But I also learned about surveying and soil sampling, and Mel and Famous were both excellent role models who knew how to have fun getting their job done. Years later, when I would see them, we still laughed about our experiences working together.

GARRISON DAM stayed in the news as a contentious topic throughout the construction period. Points of debate included a proposal for the creation of a large, government-owned for-profit company that would operate all Missouri Basin dams and sell electricity. President Harry Truman supported the idea, but in 1953, it was dead. The newly established Republican administration of President Dwight D. Eisenhower didn't like it.[18]

One year later, the dam was officially completed. Attracting curious visitors from around the world, even during the seven-year construction period, it was the largest earth-fill embankment dam in the world and still is the fifth largest. The final cost added up to $305 million, more than twice the $130 million that had been projected in 1945.

Of all the milestones in the history of the dam, one in particular impressed me: its official dedication on June 11, 1953. This was the year the dam breach was closed, water was diverted to the five tunnels, and the filling of Lake Sakakawea began, even as construction continued into 1954. The dedication drew scores of people to the area—one estimate was twenty thousand—with Eisenhower addressing the crowd in Riverdale.

Ike's speech on the dam's west embankment was something I wanted to experience up close. After volunteering to guard the Underwood Commercial Club's food stand during the night leading up to it, I nabbed a seat early in the morning right in front of the speaker podium. With nothing but a protective rope between me and the stage, I listened as the president highlighted the spiritual strength of America and talked about a general need for partnerships between the federal, state, and local governments, and the private sector.

"There is always a place in our country for private enterprise," he said.[19]

The president's words impressed me so much that I decided to talk with him. At the end of his fifteen-minute speech, I got up, stepped over the rope—and was immediately restrained by members of the Secret Service. Good thing I didn't try to get closer while he was on the stage!

The next day, one of the local newspapers published a picture of me sitting in the front row before everyone else arrived. "One of the first to see Ike," the caption read.

While parts of the president's speech rang true to me, even at eighteen, I'm not sure that I could fully appreciate others. Ike said, "When we think of how far man has come in [the past] fifty years, it is almost frightening to project our minds fifty years in advance."[20]

I wasn't frightened. But boy, was he right: the progress in technology and many other areas during those fifty years and, more broadly, during my lifetime has been stunning.

When I was growing up, there was no prevention for polio. Twin girls in my high school class, Mildred and Myrtle Sayler, were infected with the virus as children. Their backs got so bad when they were adults that they had to have multiple surgeries. Both of them were in constant pain.

The roads in Underwood, back then, weren't paved. They were just gravel and dirt. Every once in a while, a road grader would smooth them out, but then it would rain and they would get muddy, and when the mud dried, the surface was bumpy again. I had a bicycle with skinny tires that could easily get in a rut, and then I'd flip and land in the dirt.

My folks' '41 Ford, which they bought right before the war started and later let me take to college, had a column-shift, three-speed manual transmission. I still remember being with my father as he backed this new car out of the Ford garage that summer day. It would be another decade before Ford put a car with an automatic transmission on the market.

In 1946, when I was eleven, only one in two hundred

American households had a TV set. My family's radio was a box with knobs and a speaker. There was no FM back then. All we could receive were a few AM stations from Bismarck and Minot, the nearest large towns.

I had a bicycle with skinny wheels.

KFYR broadcasted one of my favorite radio shows, a five-minute segment called "Of Cabbages and Kings," and a "What's the Weather" show with music by Emil Dockter in the mornings. Every day, they pulled a postcard to see who guessed the correct temperature for that morning. If your guess was correct and it had the earliest postmark, you won five dollars. Since Mom opened the post office in the mornings, she would send in a penny postcard for each of us kids, and it wasn't unusual for one of us to win this competition. The prize could buy you a lot of candy back then. A bar of Pearson's Salted Nut Roll, one of my favorites, probably cost a nickel. Another thing that was not unusual was a comment from people in town: the Miller kids won five dollars from "What's the Weather" again.

Phone lines, particularly out in the country, were still shared. Our phone, on the dining room table, would ring once, twice, or three times to indicate which household should answer the call. Of course, the line wasn't private. You could listen in on other people's conversations. Fortunately, it wasn't long before we got a private line.

Since long-distance calls used to be expensive, people were often eager to get off the phone quickly. To let the family know that we had arrived at our destination safely, we called home person-to-person for someone and then hung up as soon as someone picked up the phone.

I remember calling home from a pay phone on the day of my arrival as a freshman at NDSU to let my folks know of my whereabouts.

Dad was on the other end, with his standard greeting: "Hello. This is Ernest Miller."

I proceeded to tell him about the events of the day: how I'd arrived in Moorhead, registered at Concordia College, and had second thoughts because of the price, and how I was now at NDSU in Fargo.

But Dad interrupted me. "Son, this is confusing, and Sophie's at the prayer meeting. Just stay where you are." With that, he hung up.

Apparently, Mom remained clueless as to my location for a week or so. The next time I called home, she said, "I was wondering where you were. You should have let me know."

Since then, technology, engineering, and the sciences have advanced in leaps.

By 1955, two years after Eisenhower's speech, Jonas Salk developed the polio vaccine, and the government initiated an inoculation campaign that led to the eradication of the virus in this country. Radios became smaller because transistors were invented. TVs were everywhere and became bigger and flatter. Cassette players, Walkmans, CDs, MP3 players, cellphones, and smartphones were invented, and now we have smart speakers that follow the command of our voice. We put a man on the moon, created the internet, and use drones for warfare. Soon, computers will be driving our cars.

12.

The Year 1977: TMC Struggles to Survive

NO LINE OF BUSINESS is immune to changes occurring in technology, its market, and the bigger economy, and many of these changes can be beyond our control. Just think about the COVID-19 pandemic. Across the country, consumers stopped going to stores. Instead, we went online to order everything from our groceries to Tylenol and meals and have things delivered. The shift affected the tech industry, the shipping and trucking industry, retail, and restaurants. The faster a business adapted, the better it fared.

At TMC, change was a constant challenge, and no time was more challenging than the first few years. It is hard to imagine today, but our original cash cow, magnetic core memory, was once considered a revolutionary invention. Originally proposed by Presper Eckert, back in 1945, the technology was first implemented by a Harvard University engineer, An Wang. Being a highly reliable, solid-state invention, core started replacing vacuum tubes for computer memory as of the early 1950s.

Vacuum tubes—they looked a bit like lightbulbs—came with huge drawbacks, including size, weight, and power consumption. Eckert and Mauchly's ENIAC, with its eighteen thousand tubes, weighed over thirty tons, occupied 1,800 square feet, and used a lot of electricity. When the ENIAC was turned on, such went the rumor, the lights in Philadelphia dimmed.

Most importantly, vacuum tubes weren't reliable. A tube had an average life expectancy of a few thousand hours, again similar to a lightbulb. With thousands of tubes in one machine, it was only a matter of a few hours before one of them failed; ENIAC is said to have had a Mean Time Between Failure of only twelve hours.[21] Every time a tube went out, a technician had to come and replace it, and if a calculation was still unfinished, it had to be started from the beginning.

Hy, who started his career when tubes were still omnipresent, remembers how ERA's 1103 computer required preventive maintenance when it was first turned on. He said that a test program would run while the computer was operating under increasingly stressful conditions to weed out any incipient failures. The machine was then returned to normal operating conditions "with a high confidence of running failure-free."

Although commercially available, the ERA 1103 was still the size of a room and had a few thousand tubes that would get very hot, which, in turn, required big pumps to circulate the cooling water.

BY THE LATE 1950s, vacuum tubes were on their way out in computers, and the industry relied entirely on solid-state technology. In new machines, semiconductor transistors replaced switching tubes, much as magnetic core memory had replaced memory tubes a few years earlier.

Being on the electronics side as opposed to manufacturing, and a few years older than I, Hy was even more aware of the technological breakthroughs occurring in the mid-twentieth century.

When he started at Westinghouse, in 1953, transistors had been out a few years but weren't yet practicable, making some people feel skeptical about their future. "The Westinghouse people said transistors would never work and vacuum tubes would always be around," Hy said.

Soon afterward, the new technology was taking off. Much

smaller than vacuum tubes, transistors were a leap forward in speed, size, reliability, and energy usage. Hy said, "It was like going from a one-hundred-watt bulb to a one-watt bulb."

Transistors launched another new era in technology: second-generation computers. Up to this day, transistors are the main building blocks of all electronics. Some people see it as the most important invention of the twentieth century.

With the use of transistors and components that were shrinking in size and weight, computer mechanics and circuits also changed. In early computers, the tubes and peripherals were all connected by individual wires and had to be attached to wooden or metal frames with clamps and other methods. These circuits were bulky, heavy, and relatively fragile. Since transistors were tiny, at least compared to tubes, an entire computer could now fit onto a board the size of a notepad. Printed circuit boards (PCBs), which were invented in England in the 1930s, became the norm. They consist of an epoxy glass board with a layer of copper foil. Through a photographic process, circuitry lines are applied to the copper. The copper between the lines is removed with etching. Components are then soldered to the board to complete the assembly.

ABOUT A DECADE after the invention of the transistor, another novelty shook the industry and made third-generation computers possible. In 1958, the year I joined UNIVAC, Jack Kilby at Texas Instruments and Robert Noyce at Fairchild Semiconductor independently came up with the idea of integrating circuitry, memory, and transistors in one small wafer made of a semiconductor material, silicon. The chip was born.

The first chips were already small and highly reliable, but they were relatively slow and expensive; as with previous technologies, the aerospace and military sectors functioned as early adopters of integrated circuits. One of the first computer models using chips was the MARTAC 420 made by Martin. The company promoted its application as ranging from nuclear reactor operations and electronic manufacturing assembly to "sending a missile roaring toward space." The computer was the size of a desk plus two filing cabinets.

By 1963, IBM and Honeywell were racing to announce new product lines with chips, and when IBM announced the System/360 series in April 1964, it was a huge marketing event reminiscent of Apple releases in more recent years. Thousands of people flocked to sales points simultaneously to hear the news. The System/360 became one of IBM's most successful product lines. More than fourteen thousand units were eventually built and sold. The largest model, called "Mainframe," cost $115,000 per month.[22]

From there, things accelerated. In 1970, one year before the opening of the plant on the reservation, Intel in California brought a memory chip to market that could read and write data like core memory. In 1971, the same company put an entire computer on a chip. Compared to the early days of vacuum tubes, this was, in Hy's words, "like going from a horse-drawn buggy to an electric car."

In a recent conversation about all these technology changes, he mentioned how chips are now produced in batch processes in silicon factories that cost billions of dollars to build. The production area needs to be sealed off and cleaner than the cleanest operating room because, as Hy said, "A speck of dust would destroy the product."

GIVEN THE FAST PACE of the sector, core memory, our first product on the reservation, had a remarkably long run. Even two decades after its invention, it was still mainstream—though it was by then obvious that the silicon chip would replace it.

As I watched the capacity of memory chips grow and their price per kilobyte come down in the mid-1970s, I grew increasingly concerned about our future. Successful during our first year—our sales were $1 million, and we made a profit—we had quickly satisfied our debt with MDS without going to the bank or anyone taking a pay cut. But the only projects that I had been able to add, like read-only memory, were small and they, too, were with MDS. My efforts to do business with Honeywell, 3M, Control Data, and other big firms in St. Paul kept failing. Our plant was far away, and there was no track record for our reliability other than MDS. Add to this that the Twin Cities' status as pre-eminent tech hub was waning. Much of the creative energy had moved west to the birthplace of the electronic chip California.

One comment that I kept hearing from potential customers as I made my sales rounds was "We love what you're doing with the plant on the reservation. We just wish we could get minority credit if we purchase from you."

Public agencies as well as large corporations generally have goals for purchasing from minority-owned businesses, but TMC wasn't in this category. Neither I nor Bob have any Native American blood in us.

To help ensure the future of TMC and the jobs that it offered, Frank, Jim, Cornelius Grant, and a few other enrolled members of the Turtle Mountain Band of Chippewa had an idea: to create a distribution company that could qualify as a minority company. They initiated the formation of Chiptronics Incorporated, which allowed our customers to buy TMC-manu-factured electronics from a minority-owned company.

There were, of course, detractors in government agencies that tried to challenge the arrangement. But the procurement people went after them, pointing out that the products were being built by Native Americans on a reservation.

Chiptronics was formed in 1977. By the summer of that same year, core memory was finally dead. My workforce, which had been at sixty when we started, was down to nine people, and three of us were engineers. It was reckoning time.

Part C:

Dealing with Setbacks

13.

A Willingness to Improve

SETBACKS, LIKE CHANGE, are a given in every business story, much as they are in every personal story. The question is how we respond to what comes our way. Can we be honest about our own limitations but focus on our assets and possible solutions? And do we just give up, or do we look for a way to manage or improve the situation and try to find a way out?

The setback that I experienced as most unsettling was health related.

I was at Atron when I ruptured a disk in my back while lifting a heavy box of printed circuit boards from the trunk under the floor of the station wagon. I felt something go. A few days later, my leg hurt, and then the pain persisted. My primary care physician prescribed exercises and sent me to the hospital to get my back stretched with weights, but nothing worked. After finally getting to the core of the problem with a CT scan, they said, "We can fix this with surgery."

"Okay. Can we do it today?"

When I woke up after the surgery, people said they could hear the relief in my voice. In the months leading up to it, the pain had been so bad that I couldn't sleep. It was a stressful time.

While the problem with my back put me in touch with my limitations like nothing before, other challenging situations felt more within my control. What's the story about Pavlov's dogs? With positive feedback and practice, they may learn new tricks.

That was me. As a high school kid in Underwood, I had little natural athletic talent but still played football and basketball. My build—I was six feet tall and probably weighed 175 pounds—helped with both, as did my willingness to learn and improve, and, of course, the teams' constant need for more bodies. There were only ninety-five students in the entire high school, and half of them were girls. If you were male and had a pulse, you were good to go.

Learning about position and strategy, I eventually became a reasonable defensive player in basketball, and I think that I did okay going after rebounds. Then again—as an underclassman, I often found myself sitting at the far end of the bench. When the band played during halftime and the team was in the locker room, I'd get an assignment: "Hey, Miller, you go play the tuba!" It was a good indication of my contribution to the team.

Football sometimes was a bit physical for me, especially without a face mask; every hit in the nose deterred me from acting aggressively for a few plays. I also wasn't fast, which is why some took to calling me "Lightning." When a story in the *Minot Daily News* about one of our games mentioned me and good play, I thought they must have gotten the wrong number.

One time, during a game on the Fort Berthold Reservation, I was knocked out from a hit to my left eye. Our coach back then was star player Clifton "Zoonie" McLean, who was later inducted into both the North Dakota and the Montana sports halls of fame. I remember coming to on the grass with Wesley Sayler, whose one eye shot off to the side, leaning over me.

"Coach," he called, "Tip's eye is out of joint!" When Zoonie arrived, all he said was "Was it a fist? Was it a fist?"

Father Dolan, who had driven to the game in his own car, took me, still in my uniform, straight from the field to the reservation health center where a doctor lanced and drained the egg-shaped swelling and then discharged me with a bandage around my head.

Meanwhile, our student manager had taken my street clothes from the locker room onto the bus with him to Underwood. When the team arrived home, he stopped at my house and pounded on the door. "Mrs. Miller, these are Tip's clothes," he said.

"Where's Tip?"

"Oh, he's hurt badly. Father Dolan is bringing him back."

The team did own one leather helmet with a face mask. After my injury, I wore it, and I became a more aggressive football player. Since there were no rules about grabbing the face mask, I would end up with a pretty stiff neck some days.

In Boy Scouts, I continued to collect merit badges even after my trip to Valley Forge. While I had no problem earning more than the twenty-one badges required for Eagle Scout, I had to stop short of pursuing this highest rank because of my very limited skills as a swimmer.

To progress up the Boy Scouts ranks, I had to pass a first-class requirement of swimming one hundred feet. There were no swimming pools within fifty miles and few lakes, and no one in my family was a swimmer. Mom had even seen somebody drown years ago, which made her fearful.

In fact, drowning accidents weren't uncommon in our area. My football teammate Wesley Sayler died in the water. Working in the field on a hot summer day, he felt the need to cool off, took an inner tube out to LeRoy Dam, fell in, and couldn't save himself. We were all shocked by Wesley's death and felt for the Sayler family.

I learned to swim from a returning veteran and local school-teacher from Underwood, Jerry Blake, who took me out to a pool in one of the mined digs at Simenson's coal strip mine.

"Keep your head back and then just paddle on your back," Jerry said.

The water was spring-fed and freezing cold, and I kept paddling until my head was stuck in the mud on the other side.

Over the years, my swimming improved a little—but the swimming and lifesaving badges required for the rank of Eagle Scout were beyond my reach.

The summer I graduated from high school, I learned that my mechanics skills also weren't quite as advanced as I may have previously thought. We became a two-car family after my folks purchased a '51 Ford with an automatic transmission. By then, I had been driving for a couple of years, because kids back in the 1940s and 1950s could get a driver's license at fourteen. (This law was especially helpful to farm families, who needed every truck driver they could get.) They gave me their old '41 Ford.

While Dad was always working and not around much for my sports activities, he did take the time to teach me about mechanics. Since he was hardly an effusive person—though he did commend me after I sang a solo at Wesley Sayler's funeral— I was used to him not saying much about any work I did. One day, however, after watching me put on new brake pads, he said, "That's pretty good, Son."

What I wasn't good at was carburetor tune-ups. Sharon and I were on our way home from a trip to the state fair when the float valve on the carburetor got stuck. I had just given the carb a tune-up. Now, I had a gas leak, which, of course, was a fire hazard.

Sharon was a fearless young woman, but when she noticed the smell of gas, she said, "I'm frightened."

I retrieved the tire iron from the trunk, gave the carburetor a good whack, and we proceeded home with the car running just fine and no gas smell. That the car should not leak gas was important to me, too: the gallon cost sixteen cents, and I didn't want to waste money.

Years later, after Pat and I signed the contract with Elmo to purchase our first home, I learned about another of my limitations: the area of woodwork. We did great with painting the house. But staining and varnishing the wood was a different deal. Until we moved to our next house years later, I would lay in bed and notice the nail holes that I hadn't filled properly. No one ever commented about the flaws that I was seeing, but I decided that we can paint but should leave the woodwork to the professionals.

14.

Meeting Challenges with Creativity

WHEN TMC HIT its low point, I still saw hope, had faith, and assumed that we would find a way to succeed. My optimistic outlook was rooted in experience, which is always an invaluable asset. As an engineer, I had spent most of my adult life doing what engineers do: design and build new things and work to solve problems. In my many jobs in Underwood and St. Paul and in student leadership positions at NDSU, I had built teams and interacted with many different types of bosses.

Among the numerous people I worked for before starting TMC, there were many I admired for their leadership qualities and others that I viewed more skeptically. One way or another, however, I learned from them all. Mel and Famous taught me, at least indirectly, that it's okay to have fun when you're in charge. Other bosses acted as role models in their interactions with their customers, local institutions, and me.

Growing up, I enjoyed being around Bud Scott, who produced the *Underwood News* and recruited local kids to catch papers off the press. He'd stand on a stool to feed the papers into the press, and I'd catch them as they came out on the other end, making sure that they stayed nice and flat. I also liked watching him set by hand all the letters to make up the words for the articles. Later, of course, he purchased a linotype machine—and gave me a lead slug off it that said "Tip Miller."

Bud always treated us with respect and continued to show an interest in our lives long after we had left town. "What's going on in college?" he would say when we returned for visits. By that time, he was very hard of hearing, so we'd have to holler.

Other times, he would pick up information about us and run a blurb in the paper: "Tip Miller, now a Senior at North Dakota Agricultural College, motored home for the weekend. He's doing well and received a scholarship."

Next thing, people in town were congratulating me. "Tip, I read about your scholarship. Great going!"

And I would explain to them that the scholarship had one criterium only: your father must have served in World War I. I think it was twenty-five dollars, and I received it every year.

One of the most demanding Underwood people I worked for was a Norwegian contractor by the name of John Torske. In high school, I ran a one-bag mixer for him that produced two or three wheelbarrows full of concrete. After I emptied a one-hundred-pound bag of cement into the mixer, I used a Ford tractor with a front-end bucket to add sand, gravel, and, of course, water. The machine mixed everything and then I emptied the concrete into wheelbarrows, which another worker picked up and wheeled to the dump spot.

There was no messing with John Torske.

One time, the kid hired to run with the wheelbarrow that day, Jimmy, arrived at the construction site early and was sitting in his car with a cigarette, waiting for the clock to start.

"What are you doing here?" John asked him.

"I came to work."

"Then why aren't you working?"

"It isn't time to start yet." John fired Jimmy, and now I was running the mixer and the wheelbarrows, too. That's when I started spreading the word: "If you go to work for Torske, don't just sit there and look! Get out and do something."

Another time, John hired me and a friend of mine to clean up the basement of a new house he was building so he could pour the basement floor. We spent a whole day hauling construction junk out, only to receive what I saw as ridiculously low pay.

Later that day, I was sitting in the shoeshine chair down at Arnold Johnson's barbershop. Looking up from his shaving job, Arnold turned to me and said, "Tip, what's going on today?"

"Well, we emptied lumber out of Don Knudson's basement so John Torske could pour the floor. And I don't know what's the matter, but he paid us hardly anything."

Arnold mumbled, "Oh, really?" When he lifted up and uncovered the man he was shaving, it was John Torske.

It was one of those occasions where I should have stayed quiet. John kept hiring me, anyway. He liked my work.

Like in high school, I worked various jobs during my four years at NDSU.

After my freshman year, the job with the Army Corps of Engineers from the previous year wasn't available. Instead, I started working again for John, who was building a new Roman Catholic church in Garrison.

Weeks into that job, one of the guys from a large construction company, Peter Kiewit & Sons, needed survey workers with experience, something I had from my time with the Army Corps of Engineers.

John was upset when I left. "I held a job for you," he said.

His team did excellent work, was in high demand in the area, and I learned a lot from him. But I needed to make all the money I could during the summer break, and surveying with a big construction company meant better pay than being a laborer.

My goal, back then, was to lighten the financial burden on my parents and be self-sustaining. As a student from North Dakota, I paid thirty-nine dollars a quarter for tuition, which was much less than the fifty-nine dollars for out-of-state kids like Pat but still a good sum.

Much as I tried, I didn't quite make it. Every once in a while, the teller at the bank in Underwood, Quentin Sayler (aka Scobuck), would say to Mom, "Tip's checking account is getting a little low." Then I'd get an infusion.

One day, I asked Dad about this. "I feel bad that I couldn't pay for it all."

"Don't," he said. "Yours was not bad compared to what it cost for your sisters."

Money aside, every job came with a learning experience.

Throughout my four years at NDSU, I was engaged on campus in paid part-time jobs and volunteer positions. For a while, I was the breakfast cook at the student union on campus, which meant getting up early to fry eggs and prepare toast for the students.

Similar to Mel and Famous Preisinger in Underwood, Cousin Pete Gjertson, who was a few years older than I and had been in the Navy, liked to have fun with me. Being a kid fresh out of high school, I was the perfect target for any mischief he could possibly come up with.

One time, there was a Coke bottle sitting on Pete's desk. I grabbed it, as I had often done before, and took a swig. The soda was spiked. I think it was my first drink of alcohol. And Pete was sitting there with a big grin on his face.

Another time, I scrambled out of bed one morning, still feeling confused as I dressed for my job as a breakfast cook. *Seems mighty early*, I thought.

Outside, it was cold, and no one was around. But I made my way across campus—only to find the doors locked when I arrived at the student union. I walked over to one of the dorms where they had a pay phone, and called up Mrs. Anderson, the manager of our cafeteria, the Bison Room. "Mrs. Anderson, there's nobody around. And we have to get ready for the students to come."

"Tip, don't you know what time it is?"

Cousin Pete had set my clock ahead two hours.

One of my first part-time positions as a student in Fargo was as a janitor at a downtown department store where I eventually got sucked into selling men's clothing. After that, I moved across the street to a men's clothing store.

The owner of the store was Myer Shark, a son of immigrants from Lithuania. His father had left Europe in the early years of the twentieth century and was now a successful businessman in Devil's Lake, North Dakota, near one of the big reservations.

One time, after attending a meeting at the local chamber of commerce, Myer vented his anger about the organization to me. They had created a list of credit-worthy people in the area but put an asterisk beside every Native American name. "I told them I'll resign from this chamber of commerce, if they don't take those asterisks off the people," he said.

This worked. The asterisks vanished.

Myer, who had earned a law degree from the University of Minnesota, was a top salesman. Whenever I had nothing else to do around the store, I stood behind the coat rack and listened to him as he persuaded people to buy a pair of pants, a shirt, or a suit. Often, those customers were of Scandinavian descent, and he would tell them, "I'm a Norwegian Jew, so I've been around here a long time."

Myer understood, and modeled for me, the importance of customer satisfaction. One Christmas, as I was leaving the store to make the 250-mile trip home, he asked if I could deliver a gift shirt ordered by one of his longtime customers in Harvey. Harvey was quite a detour, but I obliged.

CREATIVITY AND A CAPACITY to adapt, or even pivot, are skills that I first saw in my parents and mentors in Underwood. By working many different jobs and by taking on leadership positions in college, I further sharpened my own ability to respond to challenging situations—even if I sometimes felt uncertain about the best course of action.

My sophomore year, I started taking on leadership roles on campus when I signed up to be a proctor—what would now be a residence assistant (RA)—in charge of half of the dorm floor on which I lived. The position came with obligations and privileges. Different from other students, who used a large shower/bathroom for the half floor, proctors had a private room with shower and bath. I also had a master key to unlock all the rooms.

My weekly duties included handing out the mail to the students and hauling clean sheets up to the floors when the maids came once a week to change the beds. More generally, I was to keep things orderly on the floor. This meant getting kids straightened out and into bed when they had had one drink too many at a rush party. It also meant enforcing NDSU's policy of zero alcohol in the rooms.

I have to admit that I never really knew how to police such situations. On one occasion, where a few students were about to pour themselves a big glass of whiskey as I walked into their room, I took the bottle and poured it down the drain. They were veterans of the Korean War, so maybe this was a bit risky on my part. But they knew the rules and my job assignment.

While alcohol policies were strict back then, smoking was in no way prohibited or frowned upon. The student newspaper at NDSU, the *Spectrum*, featured two or three ads for tobacco products in every issue. In one advertisement that I have kept, the tobacco company Liggett & Myers invites potential buyers to "live a little!" and promises that Chesterfield King cigarettes will deliver "full-flavored satisfaction" and "BIG, BIG pleasure."

Back then, there were no health warnings on tobacco ads or products—and dorms featured cigarette vending machines. One night, as I was coming home late, I noticed that our machine was missing from its usual place in the entranceway on the first floor. Following some tracks on the linoleum floor that indicated where someone had slid the machine into one of the rooms, I opened the door with my key. My machine was right there, as were two guys, who were trying to pry it open with a hammer and a screwdriver as they stood on top of a desk.

Standing face-to-face with these students, I summoned all the authority I could muster as a nineteen-year-old proctor. "Hey guys, I think it's best to just put that thing back where it was." And they did.

In other instances, proctoring meant dealing with animals from the agriculture school. One night, I had to remove a live turkey that was jumping around in one of the dorm rooms. Another time, I was called to our TV and study room because three sheep were baaing there.

I got creative. At the end of the hallway lived a married couple that had fenced off an area outside their entry door for their child to play in. When my attempts at ushering the sheep toward that area proved fruitless, I carried them, one by one, and set them down within the fence. I can't remember what happened after that, but somehow the sheep were taken care of.

15.

Inspiring Others

IN THE FRATERNITY, we were always encouraged to be active in student leadership, and so I ran for the student senate as a junior and for the position of student body president the following year. With the senate race, it probably helped that I already knew a lot of people; I had connections as a proctor in the dorms and from the choir and the Greek system. Other students remembered me from my gig as a breakfast cook. I was elected and appointed as the commissioner of athletics.

Since the Bison were playing poorly—the football team had a terrible record—the first thing to do was ask the athletic director how we might solve the sports crisis at NDSU. He suggested a bigger budget, and so I promoted a one-dollar increase to the athletics activity fee, I believe from three dollars to four dollars. The fee, which allowed students to attend all sports games at no charge, hadn't been raised in a while, but when the increase went through, many students complained bitterly.

"Another dollar? What are you talking about?"

Learning from their complaints, I suggested a few additional changes, like attaching school events to big names. For our sports banquet in the spring, an alum serving on the athletic staff, Cliff "Bony" Rothrock, helped book Elroy "Crazylegs" Hirsch as our guest speaker. Hirsch was an idol on campuses nationwide. In 1946, he had led the college all-star team to a 16 to 0 victory over the reigning pro-football champion, the Los Angeles Rams.

Our goal in featuring him, as with some later ideas, was to help elevate school spirit and create more publicity about Bison athletics. If sports at NDSU were to improve, we needed what one might now call community buy-in.

THE RACE for student body president the following year ended with a run-off. My competitors were friends of mine: Don Schwartz and Duane "Dewey" Swenson. Both had served in the student senate and were very well-known. Neither of them was an engineer, and it had been a while since my school had last represented the student body, so I thought, *Well, here's my chance.*

Flanked by campaign managers Dick Monson (left) and Gene Stockman (right).

Thanks to my campaign managers, Dick Monson and Gene Stockman, who were both a year younger than I, I was able to win this race, too. They helped organize events to promote my candidacy and made fliers with cartoons that showed me with a cowbell. This was a reference to my participation in the Rahjah Club, which was all about getting students fired up to support our teams.

Being the student body president gave me another chance to help improve our sports program, which was doing even worse than the year before. In the late summer, I, along with others, was asked to join a meeting with NDSU president Fred Hultz. There, we learned from the athletic director, Luverne Leslie Luymes, that the football coach had resigned.

Our campaign poster.

"There's no one to replace him," Les said, adding more bad news. Only about a dozen football players would be coming back. Now, they wanted to cancel the football season.

"We can't do that," I said. "Our students work all summer somewhere in the middle of North Dakota, and all they want to do is to get back, go to the football games, and see their friends."

Somehow, we managed to convince Les Luymes to coach the team. With the help of our registrar, we went through the student roster to see who had played football before and then sent off some guys for recruiting. I remember that they even started to feel my muscles, but there was no way I was going to play college football.

My senior year was certainly my busiest college year. I had to get my degree in engineering, work to make money, serve as the student body president and chairman of homecoming, and I still had the ROTC program.

One of the more surprising things about the advanced ROTC program, which was voluntary for juniors and seniors, was the manners training. Officers were expected to show respect and comport themselves with dignity in any circumstance, including social events like a New Year's Day party at the general's house or tea with the school president and the commander of the ROTC program. And so, we learned how to hold a coffee cup and saucer in one hand and other important social manners—in addition, that is, to the outstanding leadership and military training that sets the US forces apart from others.

My first appearance as student body president was at freshman convocation, which was the culmination of a newly instituted event, freshman orientation. Female members of the Student Senate had pushed for its creation the previous year when they realized that new students needed a warmer welcome than just aptitude testing. Having myself come from a high school class of nineteen out in the country to a much bigger place, I certainly understood the need for it. In my short address in Festival Hall, following a speech by NDSU president Hultz, I shared with the assembled freshmen Mom's mantra, "If you don't have time to say hello, you're too busy."

"I think it's important that each of us recognize the other," I said. "And so, I'm going to try as much as I can to say hello to you guys and greet you. And I hope that you will do the same to me. Let's try it right now!"

I did as promised, and they responded as I had hoped.

AS STUDENT BODY PRESIDENT, I was also chairman of the homecoming committee. In the planning phase, we were on the lookout for creative ideas that could help us draw attention to our sports teams. One idea—I think it came from a good friend of mine in the engineering school, Gailon "Red" Sundseth—was to organize a torch run from Bismarck to Fargo that would arrive in Fargo just in time for the runners to join the homecoming parade.

Another, more outlandish, idea was related to the most important part of homecoming, the football game against South Dakota State University. In preparation for that day and evening, a group of students from both universities met early in the school year at SDSU in Brookings. As we discussed the role of our homecoming royalty and the game, someone came up with the idea that the student body presidents should enter a bet. And so it happened; Dave Christensen, who was my SDSU counterpart as student body president, and I bet our pants on the game.

Given the sad state of our football team, I did wonder, *What are my odds of not losing my pants in the middle of our football field?* But I was in. While I was not blessed with athletic talent, I love sports. And I was willing to do whatever it took to help promote them at NDSU and get everyone excited.

The torch run went well—a small prairie fire that one of our runners ignited was fortunately doused right away—and we received nice coverage. Part of our media strategy had been to invite the governor of North Dakota, Norman Brunsdale, to light the torch on the steps of the state capitol in Bismarck.

When a Fargo Chevy dealer wanted to participate, even more attention was guaranteed. "We'll send out three or four of our new station wagons to accompany your runners," they said, referring to the 1957 Chevrolet, which had just arrived in the showrooms. "And we'll broadcast hourly updates on the run via a local radio station, WDAY."

On the day, groups of runners took turns in the event, all wearing Bison track attire. Since the public was kept informed of the location of our runners, people stopped to watch them go by. In the small towns, the schools let out the kids for a few minutes to let them watch and wave as our students passed through.

One of the lead runners was my good friend Syl Melroe, whom I had met through the fraternity. An athletic guy and a close relative of the family that started the Bobcat Company, he was on the NDSU track and basketball teams. The 198-mile run ended with him placing the torch in the hands of our homecoming queen, Gloria Lloyd.

The parade was impressive as it went from campus down Broadway to downtown Fargo. It included many marching bands, floats representing campus organizations, and the Army and Air Force ROTC students who carried the colors.

The day was topped off by a Bison win on the football field. What a relief! I didn't lose my pants.

The next issue of the *Spectrum* reported extensively on the torch run—but it opened with an article about the bet between Dave and me, titled, "The Pants Tell the Story."[23] The accompanying image showed two young men standing in the middle of the football field. I'm on the left, hands tucked into my coat pockets, and Dave is on the right, with his shoes on the ground between us and his pants already down to his knees. The *Spectrum* write-up included what they called a "play-by-play account of the fête."

In the words of the reporter, Clark Schenkenberger, "Tip Miller strolled nonchalantly out onto the field after the final gun had sounded with the score 26-9 in the Bisons' favor. A low murmur escaped from the crowd as Dave made his appearance on the opposite side of the field. Would he actually take off his pants was the question on the lips of everyone. Now, a sigh of relief comes from the crowd and a big grin spread across Tip's face, for Dave has shed his coat. Now, the contents of his pockets followed by his shoes. Oh, my gosh, he is loosening his belt, and, and, and, and there they go!!!"[24]

He Lost His Pants: Dave Christensen (right), student body president at South Dakota State College at Brookings, lost a ...st his pants to John (Tip) Miller (left) ...dy president at ...hristensen gave ...h atmosphere at ...rs cheered.

bet Saturday as the Bison defeated the Jackrabs.

The *Forum* published the pants story in their October 28, 1956, issue.

A picture on one of the following pages shows me holding Dave's trousers up in the air, trophy-style.[25]

Publications beyond the *Spectrum* also reported on the events of the weekend. *Parade* magazine, which came with the *Minneapolis Sunday Tribune*, sent a photographer to take pictures of the torch runners out on the prairie. And the *Forum* in Fargo also published an image of the pants scene, on page one.

But nothing matched the enthusiasm at NDSU over home-coming weekend. The *Spectrum* lauded our team, which included my former competitors Don Schwartz and Dewey Swenson, for its creativity and organizational skills. President Hultz spoke in an open letter to the student body of "a project long to be remembered." He called the torch run sheer genius and commended "the never-quit spirit" of the football team.[26] And visitors from SDSU thanked us for making them feel welcome.[27] The hard work that our team put into the event had paid off.

16.

Working as a Team

AMONG MY MANY BOSSES with high standards was the person I learned from the most as an employee: my mentor at UNI-VAC, Arnie Hendrickson. Arnie modeled good leadership, which is that the person at the top of a company must have a clear picture of what the future holds, communicate it, and make things happen with courage and confidence. "We can talk about it, but here's what I believe we should do."

At least two levels above me, Arnie was a gifted technology manager. He oversaw a team of about 150 people, had everyone work in the same location, and encouraged informal communication across groups and management levels. He created synergy by making sure that everyone felt engaged, heard, and valued.

Arnie's project on which I worked as the engineering manager supervising the mechanical design was the CP-901 airborne computer to hunt enemy submarines. His team included very talented engineers. Ken Oehlers supervised the logic design, Roy Bower oversaw the memory design, Gene Giest led the power-supply design, and Larry Wozinska was in charge of the circuit design.

Almost weekly, Arnie called me into his office on the first floor of the UNIVAC building. The room was private, with soundproofing that made the silence complete when nobody spoke.

If Juel and I had a design he liked, he wanted me to push it.

"I think we should test it," he'd say.

We did, and then I'd hear, "I liked that design, but I want you to do more testing."

Arnie, who must have had a lot of experience with good and bad designs, was big on testing. His goal was to meet the customer specifications, including reliability expectations in terms of Mean Time Between Failure. The CP-901 had to survive a qualification test of one hundred failure-free hours with extreme temperature fluctuations and vibration before it was released for production. With every new test, we learned something, and had we stopped at that previous point, we wouldn't have had the success we had.

As the supervisor of the mechanical design of the CP-901, I used to travel to the Naval Air Station Patuxent River to see the P-3C aircraft and meet crew members. I enjoyed going there, and in my meetings with the officers, who were graduates of the Naval Academy with science degrees, it always struck me how excited they were about the CP-901 and how much interest they showed in the installation of the computer into the plane.

After my first visit, where I already learned a lot, we made some changes to the computer framework to make it fit better into the airframe, and after two more trips, each time with revised drawings, we agreed on the best plan for the installation. In the end, they seemed happy with the work we had done together. I know I was.

Meeting the Navy's requirements for the CP-901 computer was a challenge, and the conduction cooling of pluggable PCB assemblies was a new but exciting technology for me. Dick Ruegemer and Rudy Melzer, two staff engineers specializing in thermodynamics, shock, and vibration, ran their calculations to confirm or recommend changes to our design. Their work added confidence as we approached the qualification testing phase—and I learned again the importance of a team approach.

To make sure everyone was on the same page, we met once a week for updates on the status of everyone's work. One or more of the teams presented and explained their design, its status, and any problems on which they were working. Then we'd brainstorm to find a solution. Since there are no bad ideas in brainstorming, we'd write all suggestions down and evaluate them. This kind of teamwork made everyone see that they have a voice in the project. And having input from the entire team led to a synergy effect that often resulted in creative solutions.

The CP-901, which weighed about 380 pounds, was a big success.

UNIVAC shipped the first computer to the Navy in September 1967, and during the following two and a half decades, 498 additional units were built. Ten years ago, forty units were still being used in Japan for search and rescue missions.[28]

Today, the reliability and longevity of the Navy computers designed and built at UNIVAC are tech legend. And in the end, it was people like Arnie who established the division and its successor, UNISYS, as a favorite supplier of the Navy for years to come, thereby keeping the company on the cutting edge of technology. Because, as the saying goes, one test is worth a thousand opinions, and going forward with ideas that fail in the field can be expensive.

For me, the opportunity to work with Arnie was an invaluable lesson, both technically and on how to get things done in a large company. The process was confidence building.

Part D:

Structuring for Success

17.

An Engaged Workforce

MY PRIORITY as an entrepreneur at TMC was the same as back at UNIVAC: satisfying our customers' needs to the extent where we would be their supplier of choice. Our customers helped us get there by communicating their expectations. Their quality assurance people visited the plant and said, "Let's see your processes. What are your defects per one thousand? If there's a problem, what do you do to fix it?"

Our customers' insistence speaks to a crucial factor in running a company: the importance of having the entire organization invested in the same goals (workforce engagement). A word that I like in this context is *synergy*. If all employees know that their work contributes to the overall outcome, the total output will exceed the sum of the parts.

At TMC, I couldn't do it all myself, and Bob couldn't do it all himself. We had key areas for which we were responsible, and just as important, we surrounded ourselves with people who would do their jobs. They all had different skill sets and different levels of education and responsibility. But they all played a vital role in the production process. In the end, screwing up always hurts a company, no matter whether it happens in manufacturing, packaging, accounting, or shipping.

As CEO, I tried to ensure that our employees understood our company objective, which was to consistently satisfy or even exceed our customers' needs. I wanted everyone to be working toward this goal and feel invested in manufacturing high-quality parts and delivering top-notch service. This included being honest with the customer, a value that my folks modeled.

I remember Dad being in his early eighties and facing open-heart surgery. The night before the operation, the doctors asked him whether he had any questions.

"Yes," he said. "When I got out of the Army after World War I, they said I had an enlarged heart, and I've been receiving disability. It gets a bit bigger as I grow older. Now, you're telling me that I was born with a hole in my heart. Do I have to pay all that money back?"

Honesty was a priority for me. At TMC, my instruction to our employees was to always take customer complaints seriously without challenging their assertion that it may be our fault. "Have them return the product or get it fixed as soon as possible," I said. "Later, after we have had the opportunity to determine the cause of the problem, we can establish whose fault it was—and anyone stretching the truth with the customer is going to have a problem with me."

BE IT IN HIGH SCHOOL or in college, I was never a straight-A student. I did, however, always admire those who were. Besides being highly intelligent, they had disciplined study habits.

Pat had promised her folks that after our marriage, she would finish college. She maintained a 4.0 at the University of Minnesota while having and caring for our first child.

While I finished all my classes in the required time, a 4.0 grade point average was out of my range of possibilities. That is not to say that I didn't have high expectations of myself or even other people. I remember talking to my kids' adviser at their school one day, and she told me that our son, Mike, was doing great in math. "He's outstanding," she said.

This didn't compute with my impression of his interest or current skill level.

"Well," she said, "in the class he's in, we're happy if they can balance a checkbook."

I was stunned. "We're happy if he can balance a checkbook? I am an engineer. And that is not the level at which I want him involved."

Following this conversation, Mike, although happy in his original class, was moved to a different one. He started working for TMC a few years later, where he was responsible for company computers and procurement and met my expectations by doing a great job for us. As it turned out, he is a computer and accounting whiz.

WHILE I'VE RARELY met a business owner or manager who enjoys having to confront employees or resolve problems between them, it seems a given that disagreements will happen in any company. A lesson for me has been that every team, no matter its size, needs steps and rules for their resolution. A good manager is able to communicate these rules, handle conflict in a constructive way, not let it fester, and put their foot down when it gets too bad.

At UNIVAC, I had just been made engineering manager when I received a request from marketing: "Please send someone out to Washington, DC, who can talk with the Navy about the input/output circuit design."

I asked the group supervisor to fly to DC. We ordered his tickets for the 7:00 a.m. flight and gave him his cash.

The next morning, I was sitting in my office when the engineer who was supposed to be on the way to DC walked by. I called him in.

"Why aren't you in DC?"

"I got home last night to have dinner with my wife and told her that I really don't feel like going out there. We flipped a coin, and it came up as no trip."

To say that I was disappointed with the group supervisor for making such a decision was an understatement, and I let him know this. He should have at least called me so that I could potentially find another engineer for the trip. When I called the man who had requested engineering support to let him know about the change, he said they would handle the issue somehow. But the relationship between me and the group supervisor never returned to the pre-incident level of trust.

At the time, I was unaware of any personnel management training for engineers, but given the opportunity for a do-over, I would call Gordy Bourne, the ex-Marine personnel representative who recruited me, to come down to my office so the three of us could hash it out. I suspect it would have been an interesting discussion.

With Juel Peterson (right).

An experience at Atron that dealt with a conflict between employees proved equally enlightening. One day, a direct report of mine walked into my office. "John, you must ask Juel to talk to one of his engineers. Our assemblers are complaining how the guy smells."

Juel was also a direct report of mine—and he couldn't stand conflict. "I cannot do that," he said when I approached him on the topic.

Feeling reluctant to confront the engineer with the odor problem myself, I called in the person who had alerted me to the problem. "I was talking to Juel," I said. "We both have a problem with talking to the guy who is creating the problem. Why don't you take care of it?"

He looked at Juel and me. "Bleep you," he said and walked out the door. I guess he thought if you're in a management position, you should be able to tell people to take a bath.

The experience led me to the conclusion that it is best to handle the issue of conflict when it first occurs, involving the supervisor if necessary. This way, the issue can't fester and will stop before more levels of leadership have to become involved.

In other situations, managers need the courage to draw a line. At Atron, there was a guy in the shipping department who was very good at shipping but had a mouth that wouldn't stop. His behavior bugged me. He knew everything better and would go behind our backs to question and deride decisions that had been made.

Unfortunately, he always found an audience. While any listener could have stopped his ranting, some people chose to hear him out. Then they'd call me. "John, what's going on down there?" I asked the guy's boss, who was my direct report, to make the loudmouth shut up, but that didn't help, either.

One day, I was talking about the situation with my pastor. "John," he said, "I know I'm in the business of changing lives, but sometimes the best indicator of future performance is past performance."

When my direct report eventually had a heart attack,

leading me to wonder how my problems with the guy in shipping might have contributed to his health problems, I knew that I needed to act. "I want to dismiss him," I told the personnel department.

Of course, there were objections, mainly from people who had been listening to the man. "You can't let him go," they said. "He's too valuable to the company."

"I don't want him. If he's so valuable, you can have him."

With that, he was gone, not out the door but to another department. Putting one's foot down against strong resistance isn't easy. But it comes with the job description of manager.

18.

Incentives, Training, Unions

WHEN WE STARTED at TMC, Bob oversaw all Belcourt operations as the plant manager. But as we grew, we had to restructure and broaden the leadership.

Our first change was to split out the quality department and have its manager report directly to me rather than Bob, which relieved him of filling two conflicting roles. After a while, we also found managers to lead the test engineering and production engineering groups. While Bob, without saying much, may have resisted some of the changes we made—which manager wouldn't?—he always came around, and we were able to put together a factory management team (FMT) of six or seven people.

Spreading the responsibility for good performance in this way allowed us to create incentives for our managers that made them feel invested in the overall business goals.

The bonuses were initially dependent on a manager's team performance. But after a while, I had second thoughts. What mattered for the growth of the business and for our competitiveness was the overall performance. Our bonus system needed to reflect this by being tied to a set of company goals that I established annually with input from our board of directors and summarized for the FMT on a one-page sheet.

Our FMT, which represented purchasing, manufacturing engineering, test engineering, production, and quality, thrived on this change. They were all smart people, and if things were going great in one area, but there was a problem in another, they would say, "How can we help?" Then, we'd brainstorm as a group.

In these meetings, one man in particular, Greg Berginski, often came up with great solutions. An electrical engineer with a degree from NDSU, he would stay quiet as the others suggested one idea after another. Eventually, I would invite him to break his silence. "What do you think, Greg?"

Having listened to everyone else talk, he'd be able to see the big picture. This reminded me that we don't learn much when we're talking. We learn when we're listening.

In addition to the bonus system for the FMT, we had a stock options program in which our managers and key people could participate. Options vested after five years, and if someone left the company before then, their option to purchase was canceled. The value of TMC stock was calculated annually by Bill Patty, who had developed a formula comparing financial performance of publicly held comparable companies to TMC performance. I remember our managers and options holders always paying close attention to the new number.

Finally, we had an IRA program that was available to anyone in the company wanting to make contributions and that we supported by matching funds, and another optional program, the Christmas Saving Club. It allowed our workers to opt for a slightly lower weekly paycheck in return for an extra check toward the end of the year. Most of our factory employees were women, and they seemed to really appreciate the confidentiality of this program. The saved money came in handy for Christmas gifts.

AN IMPORTANT ELEMENT in creating a quality product and being able to continuously deliver to the same standard is ensuring good workforce training. For a while, we collaborated with the State School of Science located in Wahpeton that had an outreach program for North Dakota businesses. Their faculty would come to the plant to teach our people on the floor and train the supervisors on how to continue that training.

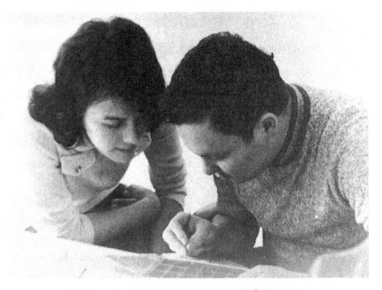

Training of a new worker at our plant in Belcourt.

At TMC, training included basic techniques like soldering—a bad solder results in a failed electronic product—and showing operators how to run machines. We had a buddy system, where experienced workers provided training and supervision for new employees and for those who showed an interest in learning new things and moving up the ranks. Since the technology was constantly changing, we made sure to push people with promise.

Among the workers showing a lot of patience with new people was Lucy Overby from Rolla, who was with us almost from the beginning. She liked to build things and was an excellent problem solver. At one point, we had a contract with UNIVAC to build cable sets. The cables were complex with tight tolerance. Lucy, who was our go-to person for this kind of task, worked with our engineers to build the first samples.

But training isn't enough. What matters just as much are the work processes. As a product went through multiple operations done by different people, I wanted everyone along the line to speak up if they saw a problem with the work in progress. "Guys, this doesn't look right. Let's talk about it and fix it."

In one such instance, we received an order for delay lines, a product made of wires and ferrite that fit well with our core-memory production. But we were having a terrible time with it. Finally, one of our supervisors sat down with the workers and said, "We're building more scrap than good product, and the customer needs good product. This must get better. I know you're capable of it. Take a week, work on it as a group, and see what you can come up with."

The workers responded with enthusiasm. They wanted to be part of a team that was successful.

OVERALL, I WORKED hard at TMC to maintain an environment where our employees had a positive attitude about the company and their jobs, and where they felt seen and valued. Once a year, we put on a corn feed for everyone. Since North Dakota doesn't have the best sweet corn, St. Paul staff brought it from Minnesota. During the party, we had drawings for small prizes. At Thanksgiving, all employees received frozen turkeys. For their birthdays, I sent them a card with five dollars and a personal greeting, and if customers visited the plant, I encouraged them to spend time on the floor with the people who were building their products. It made our workers feel good. At the end of the day, they would go home and say, "Someone from 3M came by today, and he talked with me." The same thing with politicians. One time, US Senator Byron Dorgan, a Democrat from North Dakota, made a trip to the plant. He had our people sitting on the lawn, just talking to him, and they enjoyed that.

Growing up, I never knew the party affiliation of my parents. But I started to lean toward conservatism because of other people's examples. Percy Evander, my boss in Underwood, played an indirect role in helping me find a political home. He had an addiction problem, and sometimes he would overconsume, usually when his wife was out of town. On one of those occasions, a Sunday morning, I left church early to clean the store before it opened. I found Percy had spent the night there with his dog, Pills, and needed help.

I called Dave Robinson, who was a local rancher and Percy's friend. Dave came and took Percy home, staying with him until things got better. I liked how Dave cared for his friend, and how he would take him duck hunting, which was something Percy enjoyed but was not able to do on his own. Aware that Dave and his wife were active in the Republican party—Dave served for ten years as a state legislator—I felt drawn toward conservatism.

Interestingly, one of my sisters, Colleen, who was a teacher in the Minneapolis School District, is a strong liberal and unionist. In 1970, eight years after President Kennedy, to my chagrin, signed an executive order allowing the unionization of the public workforce, she led the Minneapolis teachers on a fourteen-day strike to demand higher salaries and better benefits and working conditions.

I, FOR ONE, made up my mind to stay clear of unions when I was at UNIVAC. One day, a group of assemblers tasked with putting together a cooling system that I had designed called me to the floor.

"We have all these parts for the cooling system," they said, "and we can't put them together. Can you come over and help us?"

I showed them how to assemble the water-chilled coil and the blowers, and in the process, it seems, I picked up a tool.

Not a good idea!

Apparently, this son of a mechanic from Underwood crossed a line simply by picking up a screwdriver. Someone reported my "infraction" to the union, which filed a grievance against me for performing work that union workers are supposed to do.

The grievance was denied. Being my first personal experience with organized labor, it was still enough to deter me from engaging any further.

Later, in the early days of TMC, I received a call from a fellow manufacturer in Rugby, forty-five miles south of Dunseith. "John, have you had any pressures up there for unionization?"

"Not that I'm aware of."

"These bottom-feeding lawyers are after me," he said. "I've done everything I can, and it's expensive to fight them."

I thought, *Oh boy*, but at TMC there were no attempts at unionization. When I look at how the numbers for organized labor in the private sector have decreased over the past four decades, from about 20 percent participation to about 10 percent, I have one explanation: business owners have been working hard to meet employee needs.

19.

Adapting to Ever-Changing Production Processes

A FEW YEARS after I started TMC, one of the most influential business books ever written hit the market: *In Search of Excellence* by Tom Peters and Robert H. Waterman Jr. There, I discovered information that helped guide my perspective as an entrepreneur: Knowing the business you're in matters more than knowing how to run a business. An MBA degree is not a requirement for success.

As I managed TMC—without an MBA—I was keenly aware of the lessons I learned from being a part of the NTDS and CP-901 projects and how my experience with this ambitious, risky, and complex undertaking set me up perfectly for the manufacturing sector. I understood the importance of maintaining a close and collaborative working relationship between customer and supplier, and I knew that quality and dependability are key.

Even in its early years, the NTDS project was recognized as highly successful. In 1962, President Kennedy set up a commission to investigate why so many military projects were failing. When he asked the group to showcase the two most successful projects in every branch of the service, they selected NTDS for the Navy.[29]

Since the Navy projects were constantly pushing the technology, I had a competitive edge with TMC. Based on my work with UNIVAC, I could give commercial customers recommendations that might improve their equipment. And their engineers could feel confident that I was experienced with types of technology with which they might not yet be familiar.

At the same time, the evolution in technology and our customers' ever-changing needs profoundly impacted our production processes. When we started operating on the reservation, components such as transistors and core memory were soldered by hand to holes in a printed circuit board. Later, to increase production, flow soldering was added. And when surface-mounted components became the norm, reflow soldering was introduced.

Like other discrete components before them, early integrated circuits, known as dual in-line packages, have leads that are inserted into the printed circuit board. In second-generation integrated circuits, however, leads stretch out horizontally on all four sides. Pick-and-place machines set these flat packages onto pads on the board that are covered with solder paste, all with the help of cameras and lasers to ensure a perfect fit. The boards are then soldered in a reflow oven with nitrogen to fuse the connections. Finally, they need to be cleaned thoroughly and sent on to the testing operation.

As the technology progressed, the distance between the soldering pads got smaller, and toward the end of my career, a new surface-mounting technology appeared, the ball grid array. Now standard, it allows for hundreds of ball connections on the bottom side of the circuit—and creates a need for X-ray equipment to inspect the solder joints.

The fast-paced technology changes were exciting and challenging. We had to continuously invest in newer and more precise placement and X-ray machines, reskill our workforce, and keep up with quality-control methods. Bottom line, we were investing in the manufacturing of the latest technology while retaining the capabilities of the previous technologies.

With all this change going on, it was still important to me that I stayed with what I had learned and did well. In the early days of TMC, one of my electrical engineer friends came up with a battery-operated, pocket-size fish finder. I built a couple of those but then didn't have time to go out and market them. When another company introduced them years later, I had no regrets.

As an entrepreneur, I found it important to set boundaries for the company, especially in the start-up phase. It was a matter of "stick to your knitting." Our strength was in manufacturing parts for customers and maintaining their trust by keeping the service level high.

20.

Every Sale Starts with a Greeting: The Turnaround

AS I REFLECT on my experience at TMC during the summer of 1977, the year core memory died, I can't help but once again remember my mom's much-repeated admonition: "If you don't have time to say hello, you're too busy."

Some very good experiences in my life resulted from simply walking up to people and saying hello. A conversation might start. Occasionally, I ran into that person again, we might discover commonalities, and, in some cases, this would lead to new business.

Our son, Mike, was in youth football. On Saturday mornings, I was on the field holding one end of the ten-yard chain. On the other end, there was another dad, Mel Koshiol, who was a manufacturing manager at 3M. As we began talking, we realized that we had mutual friends.

One game day, I told Mel about TMC. As it happened, he oversaw production of 3M's library theft-detection system. Two lattices that library patrons walk through as they exit the building detected from a magnetic strip in a book whether it was checked out properly. Mel needed someone to manufacture the power supply for the system—a unique opportunity for TMC. I invited him to visit our plant, combined with a day of goose hunting, and soon we had our first 3M contract.

SHORTLY AFTER MEL'S VISIT, the EDA organized a tour of North and South Dakota reservations for representatives of major corporations. The idea was for companies like 3M, IBM, and Honeywell to explore opportunities with potential suppliers in economically disadvantaged areas. Belcourt was on the list.

With business as low as it was, Bob and I prepared thoroughly for the visit. Expecting temperatures well in the nineties, we made sure to have plenty of cold water and soda on hand. Bob, who is a good cook, put together some cold salads. Most importantly, we also found ten factory workers to make us look busy.

With the wind blowing at fifty-five miles an hour, the purchasing reps came in on a tiny plane and looked quite shaken as they stepped onto the tarmac, briefcases in hand. After a tour of the plant, we fed them and gave our pitch in the factory lunchroom that we had cooled down as best we could.

The two IBM reps—one from their Rochester, Minnesota, location and the other from Boulder, Colorado—must have liked our presentation. The Rochester guy left me with an invitation to visit him and his purchasing department for a second pitch.

The invitation in itself felt like a high point. Here, finally, was a large company representative who wanted to talk to me about business.

The 3M guy, on the other hand, returned from the EDA day to St. Paul and told his purchasing group, "I think that company is not going to survive."

At this point, Mel stepped in for us. Referencing the work that we had already done for 3M, he persuaded the purchasing manager not to pull out of our existing contract.

Following my pitch to IBM's purchasing group in Rochester, I was in for a disappointment. Over lunch in the cafeteria, I learned that our capabilities didn't fit with IBM's needs. I was about to leave the building when one of the engineering managers stopped me. "Hang in there," he said. "I'm an NDSU Bison. I'll keep my eyes open for something."

Only a few weeks later, I received a call from the fellow alum, saying that he had an opportunity that might interest me. I drove down to Rochester the next day to see what he was talking about—and already knew what my answer would be.

The following week, IBM sent a truckload of parts to Belcourt. More than 1.5 million springs, screws, nuts, and bolts had to be sorted by part number, bagged, and returned to Rochester—and this was only the first part of our contract with them. As a manufacturer of card punch and read equipment, IBM had a contractual requirement to provide spare relays for the life of government-owned equipment. Our next step in the contract was to build and test these replacement relays. We didn't make much of a profit with that deal, but it was our entry into IBM.

Both IBM and 3M became longtime TMC customers. After we proved ourselves with the current pulse generator for their library theft-detection system, 3M had confidence in our capabilities as a company and my strength in mechanical design. Their purchasers appreciated not only our pricing but also our location, which allowed them to combine visits to the plant with hunting and fishing excursions. One purchaser liked to shoot prairie dogs. Another enjoyed goose hunting. The only problem with him was his tendency to claim every downed goose as his. Of course, we kept our mouths shut.

One day, the 3M manager called me with a request for a major upgrade of their system. With the existing one, their workers were spending too much time installing the system out in the field, where they had to load separate boxes for the lattices and the base onto a forklift and assemble the components in the library.

"It needs to be more compact and easier to install," their manufacturing manager said. "Can you work with our engineers to get that done?"

The new model that we developed was almost preassembled. It fit into a single box that could be loaded onto a handcart and wheeled through a door. All a worker needed to do was slide the base and the lattices apart, tie everything together with a few screws, and plug it in.

The contract forced us, at TMC, to learn new technologies, like welding plastic, but soon we were shipping a truckload of new and improved library theft-detection systems out of North Dakota every week. The product did so well that it earned 3M's coveted Golden Step Award, given for innovations that reach a certain revenue goal in a prescribed period. While the award goes to 3M's employees, we also received a plaque.

Our relationship with 3M was one of many win-win situations. They had some very smart electrical engineers, and we had expertise in manufacturing, so our capabilities bolstered theirs. IBM, Honeywell, and others trusted us in a similar way—and we kept winning new contracts.

IBM eventually became our biggest account, making up close to 50 percent of our business, a threshold they didn't want us to pass. Since our IBM line kept expanding, this kept the pressure on us to grow our business with our other customers and to find new ones.

An interesting aspect of doing business with IBM was their insistence on open-book pricing. Their engineers could gauge well what it would cost us to manufacture a certain product, and if our bid was too high or too low, an IBM purchaser might call me. "We think there's something out of whack with your bid. Can we talk about it?"

Some of my sales guys didn't appreciate the transparency; they worried we might be leaving money on the table. But I liked it. I knew that the customer saw the price as fair, provided we did a good job, and that they would be open to discussions should there be a problem. It is true, of course, that IBM, as a supplier, would never have put up with our small profit margin.

The difference was that they dominated their market. I had multiple competitors.

HAPPY CUSTOMERS are repeat customers. They can be an asset in sales talks with other companies. And sometimes they will introduce a supplier to a new customer. IBM introduced us to Walgreens and Cisco.

Walgreens, which relied on IBM for all its computers, needed a pick-to-light system in their distribution centers for less than case-lot items. A pick-to-light system uses lights and LEDs on racks and shelves to indicate pick locations and guide pickers through their work. With their stores lacking the space to keep more inventory on hand than fits on the customer-facing store shelf, this kind of system simplifies the replenishing process on the warehouse end. IBM designed the pick-to-light system for Walgreens, and thanks to IBM's endorsement, we received the contract for manufacturing and installing the systems in their multiple warehouses.

In Cisco's case, while we satisfactorily delivered initial orders, the relationship didn't flourish. We were just too far away from their headquarters in California—in terms of geography and culture.

In addition to IBM and 3M, we eventually gained Honeywell as a customer— in spite of an incident that occurred early in my relationship with the buyer, an engineer in procurement, Gene Lehtinen.

After meeting once in St. Paul, Gene and I made an appointment for him to visit our plant in North Dakota. I booked two rooms for us at Buzz's Northern Lights Motel, a small place with very few rooms in Rolla, located just east of the reservation. Gene was going to fly up. I drove.

After leaving St. Paul somewhat late in the day, I stopped en route and called the motel to inquire whether Gene had already checked in.

"Mr. Lehtinen is here," the receptionist said and gave me my room number.

When I arrived at the motel at one o'clock in the morning, the door with my number had a note taped to it: "Mr. Miller: Sorry. I had to sell your room. Please go sleep with your guest."

The receptionist, I knew, was a good Christian. Unable to turn away people looking for a place to stay, she had obviously decided I should bunk with Gene.

Turning away from the door with the note, I saw Gene leaning out of his window and already in the know. "John, come on in!"

The room had two beds. He offered me a drink, and we laughed about the situation.

Our business line with Honeywell, which had very supportive engineers and quality-control people, included ring laser gyroscopes (RLGs) for the military. A highly accurate technology, RLGs are used in submarines, aircraft, and ground vehicles to determine and maintain the orientation of an object in space. I recently learned that Honeywell, since starting RLG production for the US Navy in 1966, has produced and shipped more than half a million RLG units. A good portion of the electronics for them must have come out of our plant in North Dakota.

Honeywell was one of many customers where I could use my early experience with military applications as a reference in sales talks. The same was true, of course, with Sperry Rand (now UNISYS), which, in 1986, nominated TMC for the Small Business Administration's Subcontractor of the Year Award.

In their endorsement of TMC, Sperry noted competitive pricing, superior customer service and responsiveness, and "superb performance" in quality control. They liked that our quality performance did not require source inspection at our plant; they could inspect upon receipt at their site. What impressed them most was our ability to quickly accommodate engineering design changes for a group of complicated cable assemblies that we manufactured for their Defense Products Group.

As our business grew, I used awards and recognitions from companies like Sperry, Honeywell, and IBM in my sales pitch. Being an approved supplier for our big business partners gave us a boost when other customers evaluated whether they should give us contracts: "You're satisfying the needs of these large contractors? You must be getting things right!"

21.

Relying on Key People

AFTER THE BUSINESS started growing, I relied even more than before on people like Bob and Pat, and, eventually, on our son, Mike.

Most weeks, I was on the road a lot, traveling back and forth between our office in St. Paul and the production facility in North Dakota, often with my station wagon full of parts to keep our shipping costs low. Tuesday through Thursdays I usually spent at the plant. Bob and our people there were all eager to do a good job and be successful. But they also needed the technical expertise that I had with electronics assembly and manufacturing. At the same time, I knew that the office in St. Paul, where we did the purchasing, contracts, and financials, was in good hands with Pat.

For me, splitting my time between the two locations worked out perfectly—and both locations seemed to like that I wasn't around all the time. Especially in the beginning, there were problems to address on both ends. I would show up, shake the grates to get things resolved, and after a few days, people were happy to see me go.

Pat, who worked from a front corner office with big windows, always felt comfortable making decisions in St. Paul. She knew how to hold people to task and had everyone's respect. Some of the women at the office called her the dragon lady and referred to her assistant, Kim, as the dragon lady-in-waiting. Kim had total faith in Pat—and neither of them had a problem expressing their opinions if they saw the need for me to do things differently.

Pat was also a good judge of character and an excellent listener. Every once in a while, she would accompany me on a trip to the plant, and the women there would tell her about the things they'd like fixed.

On our way back to Minnesota, Pat would bring up the issues. "What are you going to do about it?"

When an employee didn't deliver, she was just as quick to challenge them.

On one occasion, I contracted with a NDSU classmate to find a good salesperson. Pat, remembering this man from our college years, seemed doubtful from the start. I hadn't met him before, but he was a nice guy and had previously been a VP at Cray Research, so I paid him a handsome sum to go find good salespeople for us.

The first person he brought in was a definite no-go, and the second was even worse. By this time, Pat had already given up on him.

Finally, he found a candidate whom we hired. The first thing our new employee did, under Pat's disapproving eye, was to bring in new furniture and turn the loft upstairs into an office. Not much later, I sent this new hire to go visit an existing customer in Denver, warning him to avoid one specific topic.

"There's one issue I don't want you talking to them about. If it comes up, just tell them you're unaware of the details, and they should call me."

Then he went there and brought up the topic.

When I told Pat about the problem, all she said was "Well, you were the one who signed up my NDSU classmate to find him."

THE PART WHERE Pat and I may have complemented each other best was her ability to keep things on schedule—even when dealing with our son, Mike. Faced with his tendency for procrastination, which he must have inherited from me, she could be tough on him: "This needs to get done. When is it going to happen?"

Mike was in his early twenties when he joined our company after being in and out of college for a few years and waffling about where to take his life. What brought him to TMC was a mishap at an excavator company for which he was working.

He was out in the field, repairing a septic tank on a farm, when the wall underneath him collapsed and sent him down into the sewage. People quickly pulled him out of the mess, had him take off his clothes, and hosed him down so that he wouldn't get sick.

The next day he came to see me. "Hey, Dad, I don't suppose you have a job for me?"

"Okay. But the rules are going to apply to you like everybody else."

Mike's value to the company revealed itself after we decided to digitize our administration with a Manufacture Resource Planning system (MRP). At the end of the month, if our financial statements didn't match our expectations, he'd go around the clock to find the mistake. Simple errors like someone entering a sales price of x per unit instead of x per one hundred units can make a huge difference. Fortunately, Mike has an uncanny ability to mine information and find this kind of faulty data entry. He is still doing the same for the boss at the firm where he now works.

22.

Quality Equals Profit

BREAKTHROUGHS in computer technology weren't the only change that impacted my business. Starting in the 1980s, manufacturing companies across the nation, and in sectors ranging from automobiles to electronics, saw themselves challenged to rethink their processes because of competition from Asia, and especially Japan.

Japanese exports, known in the first half of the twentieth century for their shoddy manufacturing, rapidly improved after World War II, when companies adopted a new, quality-focused approach. The shift allowed Japan to establish itself as a major export market for cars, color TV sets, electronics, and other goods.

Not surprisingly, American efforts to respond with price reductions and import restrictions failed to change the dynamic. While the US military sector had standard specifications for quality known as MIL-Q-9858, the private sector had long failed to adopt a comparable industry standard. The quality differential remained, and by 1980, the US was running a trade deficit with Japan.

An up-close view of how market shares changed in the 1970s and 1980s reveals sobering numbers.

In 1970, US companies produced 89 percent of semiconductors, almost 100 percent of machine tools, 99 percent of telephone sets, and 98 percent of color TV sets sold in our country. Eight years later, these numbers had dropped to 64, 35, 25, and 10 percent.[30]

On June 24, 1980, a primetime NBC television show, *NBC Whitepaper*, broadcast an episode called "If Japan Can…Why Can't We?"

The show, which detailed how Japan captured the world's automotive and electronics market, ignited a fierce national debate, with everyone blaming everyone. Depending on people's viewpoint, it was the fault of the politicians, the unions, the workers, the managers, capitalism, socialism, and, above all, the Japanese.[31]

Ironically, the story of Japan's manufacturing success starts with a handful of Americans, including General Douglas MacArthur, the Allied commander of the Japanese occupation from 1945 to 1951. With local radio plants destroyed in the war, he needed production of radio sets ramped up so that his orders and the Voice of America could be heard in every home on the islands. After sending for help from the US, he gave the initiative to a twenty-nine-year-old systems and electronics engineer with experience in radio and radar, Homer Sarasohn.

Sarasohn agreed to do a review of the radio-manufacturing industry and restarted production in less than a year. This was all US-financed, but again, the quality was subpar. When the young engineer sought feedback from the managers on how to improve production processes, he encountered silence. They were culturally not attuned to being asked for input.[32]

By the late 1940s, Sarasohn was arguing that the continued production of scrap, which resulted in waste and the need for do-overs, was costly and could overburden US taxpayers. He promoted that American manufacturing know-how should be shared with the Japanese.

Not everyone liked the idea.

"We would create a monster," the naysayers warned.[33]

At the end of a meeting where both sides presented their positions, MacArthur made the final decision. "Go do it," he told Sarasohn.[34]

From then on, Sarasohn, who once said that a quality-driven approach "seemed natural" to him,[35] had total authority over the Japanese radio industry. He and a colleague from Western Electric put together a textbook and taught Japanese plant managers how to run a modern manufacturing firm. Among their pupils were the men who went on to found Sony and Mitsubishi. "As you know from history, they passed the course," Sarasohn later said.[36]

Sarasohn, who originally committed to spending nine months in Japan, stayed there five years and even learned the language to improve his communication with the country's top managers. And before returning to the US, he introduced local industry leaders to another American quality expert, W. Edwards Deming.

A quality engineer and former statistician, Deming may be considered a prophet who wasn't heard in his own land. While US military suppliers like UNIVAC were always held to a high standard, other American industry leaders refused to adopt the quality-control techniques that he suggested. In Japan, however, Deming's teachings were so well received that he was awarded the Emperor's Medal of the Sacred Treasure. And the Japanese Association of Engineers named a prestigious quality award after him, the Deming Prize.[37]

Overall, I believe that MacArthur's man in Japan, Sarasohn, had it right: the quality-first approach seems natural, is cost-effective, and makes customers happy. In fact, quality is key to the long-term success of any organization, be it private or public, profit or nonprofit, in manufacturing or service. Sarasohn also deserves respect for overcoming US fears of a rebuilt Japan as well as language and cultural barriers, and a lack of management buy-in. That said, I can understand the concerns of some about using American taxpayer money to rebuild Japan. A few years after the war, the sneak attack on Pearl Harbor, the atrocities of the Bataan Death March, and the POW camps were still on people's minds.

In hindsight, the difference between our and Japan's attitude toward quality improvement might be best explained with the effect of World War II. Japanese companies were destroyed in the war. They lost their factories, markets, and machines—everything but their workforce. They had to rebuild, and failure was not an option. American companies, by contrast, dominated the world economy after World War II and felt no imperative to change or improve until Japanese companies, following considerable US investment, began pushing them out.

THE QUALITY REVOLUTION that started in Japan spread across the world and became known by many names. Lean manufacturing evolved from the Toyota production system and is probably the best-known framework. Six Sigma was developed by US manufacturer Motorola. All approaches share a few guiding principles: quality equals profit, delight the customer, exceed customer expectations, never stop improving, respect the worker, and give workers autonomy, meaning, and training.

In 1987, the ISO 9000 was published. Recognized internationally, it contains a series of standards for quality assurance and quality management. The most popular of these standards is the ISO 9001, which addresses quality management systems and allows for certification.

In the US, also in 1987, a partnership between industry leaders and the US government introduced the Malcolm Baldrige National Quality Award. Named after the secretary of commerce under President Ronald Reagan, the award was modeled on Japan's Deming Prize.

When Reagan, who was a great communicator and one of my heroes, gave out the first Baldrige awards, in 1988, he said,

"America's economic strength depends on industry's ability to improve productivity and quality and to remain on the cutting edge of technology. That's why the Malcolm Baldrige National Quality Award is so important."[38]

Two years later, Pat and I, along with other suppliers, were invited to the event when our customer, IBM Rochester, received the award.

ONE MIGHT SAY that American manufacturers woke up to the quality-first message rather late. To this day, people will talk about their good experience with a Japanese car and how they used to drive a Ford that "needed a repair a day." Unfortunately, a damaged reputation takes time to mend; what some consumers aren't aware of is that our industry has long caught up, that Ford can now hold its own against Toyota.

Anyone pushing for quality will learn that it is hard to achieve. Getting there takes time, and the quest needs to be ongoing. For TMC, a small manufacturing company on the northern edge of North Dakota, ISO certification provided a big boost. It was a signal to the world that we had a system and practices that allowed us to consistently manufacture products that met customer and regulatory requirements, and it helped us attain approved-supplier status with big-label customers like IBM, Honeywell, and 3M.

Applying for ISO certification meant preparing dozens of documents that detailed how we ran the business. Since even the smallest piece of information was subject to audit, the effort required good judgment. Bob ran it with assistance from others, including an electrical engineer with patience for paperwork, Greg Berginski. Third-party auditors then came in to verify that we were operating the business as defined in our documents. Once we had satisfied these audits multiple times—and there could be surprise audits—the auditors approved us as ISO-certified.

Becoming ISO-certified was a major step forward and an achievement not all attain. While the process was still ongoing, we could at least state that TMC was ISO-compliant.

Driving quality standards into the supply chain is a crucial part of achieving overall quality goals. As a supplier, we received a lot of attention, education, and help on the quality topic from big customers, who tried hard to develop a partnership relationship.

The manufacturing manager at 3M, John Hamann, and his team met with us every six months for a quality review. One meeting was held annually at the 3M Center. We gave our presentations and they shared with us their charts of TMC's quality performance. Six months later, in the summertime, the 3M team came out to the plant with a similar agenda.

In 1988, Honeywell's engineers assisted us in transitioning the gyroscope line to a flow cell with just-in-time, lean methods. The training they provided resulted in a few of our employees gaining their Six Sigma green belts, a mark of their demonstrated knowledge of quality-improvement processes. We, in turn, tried to push a quality-focused partnership approach to our suppliers.

23.

Working with Sales and Purchasing People

WHEN I TALK with people who aren't in sales about the qualities and skills needed to win over new customers, I sometimes come across a misconception: that getting another person to buy something comes simply from having a convincing pitch. In my experience, giving the other person a chance to talk about their problems and needs and showing an understanding for them is just as important.

The more information I could get from a potential client, the better my chances became of moving forward with them. Sometimes, I discovered that there was no point in pursuing a deal, that it wasn't worth the effort. But other times, I learned about my counterpart's problems, and then I'd say, "I can help you with that."

Selling is a complex undertaking: there's a rhythm to it, some parts are slower or quieter than others, and timing matters.

I REMEMBER A VISIT to an irrigation company together with a sales representative with whom we worked, Norris Stricker. Norris and our engineers had been working on the proposal for a long time. All that was needed was a purchase order from the buyer.

The company, Reinke, produced an advanced type of center

pivot irrigators: while original models watered in a circular pattern, their solution featured a swing arm at the end of the irrigator boom that could fold out and back, and thereby reach into the corners of a field. Guidance for the swing arm was provided through an expensive control box purchased from a company in Chicago, and Reinke wanted us to reverse engineer the controller with updates.

As Norris and I sat with their buyer, Reinke's managers kept checking in on us. "How's it going?" From their behavior, it was obvious that they needed us and were eager for their buyer to make a decision.

A Navy boxer turned salesman, Norris knew a thing or two about timing. He let the buyer dilly-dally before saying, "We've answered all your questions. Is there any reason that you cannot give us a purchase order today?"

The room fell quiet. Norris kept his eyes on the buyer. I sat and waited, feeling the weight of the silence.

After what seemed like an eternity, the buyer turned fidgety. "I guess not," he said.

As Norris and I got into the car, purchase order in hand, I said, "It seemed to me, during that grueling minute, if I opened my mouth, you would punch me right in the face."

"You got that right, John."

MOST PURCHASERS with whom I dealt on the customer side and as TMC representatives were women with excellent interpersonal skills. They often weren't engineers or manufacturing experts but came, instead, with business training.

At one point, as I was hoping to expand our business line with 3M, I kept getting stuck in my meetings with their engineers in New Ulm, Minnesota, a very nice town with a German emphasis.

Enter a young TMC sales representative, Joanie Kulschbach.

Joanie and I first met when she tried to sign me up for the St. Paul Chamber of Commerce. I remember thinking as I listened to her pitch, *Boy, she can sell.*

When she was done, I asked her a few questions: "I'm curious, how did you get the job selling? Do you like being in sales? What kind of money are you making?"

The next day, she called me to ask whether she could interview to work in sales for TMC.

Hiring Joanie turned out to be a good move. She knew how to relate to people, and having lived in Germany for a while, she spoke the 3M engineers' language and understood their mindset. Where I was sometimes hesitant to ask questions that I thought our counterpart might not want to answer, she didn't hesitate to inquire about the project, its schedule, or any other relevant topic. She had a list of important questions to keep us in the game, and she was going to ask them.

Suddenly, these men opened up. *Maybe Turtle Mountain isn't so bad,* they must have thought. *We'll spend more time with them.*

Joanie eventually became friends with my older daughter, Lisa, and left TMC to move west. She now sells software out of the Denver, Colorado, area.

At TMC, I found that purchasers on the customer side tended to be very supportive if we delivered according to our contract, did a good job with excellent quality, adhered to schedules, or gave them a heads-up when problems arose. On the other hand, they understood their responsibility toward their employer and could also be firm, if necessary.

As the years went on, more and more women became purchasing agents, at least for our commodity, which was a contracted service. In most cases, if we had an appointment and weren't a current supplier, prospective customers were attentive to our presentation and wanted to know more about what we could do for their companies.

IN THE CASE of all customers, I used to find that a solid relationship with their engineers, quality-control people, and purchasers would go a long way. My expectation was that the people with whom I was interfacing would call me as soon as a problem arose: "John, we have this issue going on, and we'd like you to nip it in the bud."

This, of course, was as much in our interest as in theirs. No one deciding to award a big contract to a supplier wants to hear, "Gosh, they picked the wrong people to do business with." And it allowed us to stay ahead of problems that could easily get blown out of proportion by detractors who might have preferred a TMC competitor get the contract. After all, not everybody on the customer side might be my friend.

On my visits to companies with existing contracts, I'd stop at a bakery and pick up a box of doughnuts or rolls. And when a potential customer sent a group of four or five engineers and purchasing and quality-control people to check out the plant in North Dakota, we tried to exceed expectations in every way.

We made sure that everything in our plant met their production standards for cleanliness and a static-free environment and that we used equipment with which they were familiar. We talked their language of good engineering. And we introduced them to the best the region had to offer in fun, food, and entertainment.

For lunch, we all lined up at Dale's Truck Stop. If a first-time visitor asked for a recommendation from the menu, we'd suggest the King of the Road burger. When the food arrived, their jaw would drop. The burger was the size of a plate.

In the evenings, we took them up to Lake Metigoshe for a pontoon boat ride and dinner at the steak house. A pianist who was recently inducted into the Dakota Musicians Association Hall of Fame, Gordy "Crazy Fingers" Lindquist, provided the entertainment.

Gordy is a lot of fun and helped us raise our image. If I gave him the names of our guests and a bit of information about each one, he would mention them in his performance. The visitors really enjoyed this. And when he led us in the "Oklahoma" song, we all sang along with gusto, replacing Oklahoma with North Dakota.

This kind of programming did a couple of things for us.

When a colleague asked, after a purchaser's return, "What was it like out in North Dakota on the reservation?" they would have a surprising story to tell. And by bringing more of our own people together with our customers, we were expanding the relationship between the organizations. This, in turn, relieved me from having to do all the sales work.

I remember how a Denver-based purchaser who came from a farm environment enjoyed spending time with some of our employees who farmed on the side. If she needed additional work done, she wouldn't go through me but talk to them directly. I got involved only when necessary.

Somebody recently asked me whether we ever received pushback for entertaining purchasers. The answer is no, even though there were companies with very tight rules around invitations. UNIVAC, as a military supplier, is one such example. But even there, I would have been surprised if somebody was going to raise hell over a half-dozen doughnuts that I brought to a meeting. It would have been like Atron's accounting guy telling me that I couldn't give a popcorn popper to a core-memory stringer who met the one-hundred-units milestone. As for the programming out in North Dakota—what was the alternative? Unless we organized something, visitors might be sitting alone in the evenings.

24.

Banks: Surviving the Workout Group

BEING A BUSINESS OWNER can sometimes feel like riding a roller coaster. It's up and down. You solve one problem and a new one appears. In our case, the acquisition of new, high-profile customers resulted in space problems and trouble with banks.

TMC was able to avoid borrowing money for a while. After we received the IBM and 3M contracts, however, our financial needs changed: provided our customers paid us within the agreed terms, I had enough cash on hand to take care of our payroll but still needed funds to pay for the inventory.

Because of my frequent visits of the plant, I had an apartment in Rolla, on the eastern edge of the reservation, and I initially approached the First National Bank of Rolla. The banker there, Earl Locken, asked me for details: How much money did we need? When did we need it? What would our payment schedule look like?

Of course, there was no Microsoft Excel back then, but I drew up a clear and convincing spreadsheet for him.

Earl clearly must have liked my engineer-style presentation. We got the loan and made our payments as planned, always calling ahead if any changes were required. All was well—until the bank in Rolla switched owners and our plant became too small.

BY THE END of the 1970s, with business increasing at a fast clip and even more parts and inventory arriving for assembly, the storage space in our factory at Belcourt began to encroach on our work area, and IBM put pressure on me to expand the plant.

"If you don't get more space," they said, "it will limit how much business we can do with you."

By this point, the tribal council had already doubled our factory area to seven thousand square feet. When I approached them on the topic of additional space—Jim Henry was no longer in charge—their new leader blew me off.

"If you need more space, you build it," Wayne Keplin said.

It seems that Wayne and I were not a good fit, though I sometimes wonder whether his opposition had less to do with me and more with our use of the word *corporation* in the company name. The perception that corporations don't pay taxes was pervasive in some circles, even back then.

Add to this a rivalry between different groups on the reservation. After the creation of Chiptronics, there was talk about Jim's involvement with TMC and how he might be receiving kickbacks. This was not the case, but even false rumors tend to die hard.

Not interested in investing on the reservation and being governed by tribal regulations, I opted, instead, to move TMC. In Dunseith, a small town just west of the reservation, we found a city-owned 12,500-square-foot building that stood empty. Still lacking air conditioning, it was an open shell with a concrete base and required some capital investment. But it was brand-new, basic plumbing was in place, and the site was eligible for a federal Urban Development Acceleration Grant (UDAG) amounting to a couple hundred thousand dollars.

Enacted in 1977, during the presidency of Jimmy Carter, UDAG grants were designed to stimulate the economies of distressed cities and urban counties. The money went to the City of Dunseith, which used the funds to make the necessary investments for TMC to move into their vacant building.

THE DEDICATION of our new plant, which we celebrated with a pig feed for our employees, customers, and other stakeholders, brought an unpleasant surprise. After they were done eating our pork sandwiches, the new owners of the bank in Rolla wiped the drippings off their fingers and said, "We don't want to do business with you anymore."

Their decision, I believe, was based on a combination of factors. They felt skeptical about us relying on a reservation-based workforce, and Earl, who had always trusted me to succeed, had unfortunately left the bank.

In need of a new lender, I called Earl, who was now at a family-owned bank in Rugby. He was happy to add us to his list of customers, but as our requirements grew, a long-term relationship was not meant to be. Apparently, one of the bank owner's sons didn't like the idea.

Earl, who had to deliver the message to me, advised me to approach First National Bank in St. Paul. In the long run, this turned out to be a boon because they had the money to do whatever we needed to do. But in the short run—again, it was a bumpy ride.

We had been in Dunseith a few years when I bid a project with the Donaldson Company, a Minnesota-based manufacturer of air filters, mufflers, and other components to be used in trucks and tractors. At the time, they were planning to launch a new electronic product, a noise-measuring device that allows highway patrol officers to determine whether a truck engine is too loud.

As we drew closer to a deal, Donaldson's purchasing people asked me to bring in my financial statements. I saw no problem with this; after all, we had been profitable for a while. But soon I had an appointment with their finance department.

"We see you have a couple hundred thousand dollars in receivables from Time Management Corporation," they said.

"We're worried that you might not get that money, and if you don't get it, you might not be in business for us."

I was stunned. I had been talking to the Time Management CEO, and they seemed to be doing just great.

But the Donaldson purchaser was adamant. "It doesn't look good to us," he said. "You can't have our business."

Next thing I knew, Dave Peterson, my banker in the mighty First National Bank tower in downtown St. Paul, asked me to come in. Apparently, he was suddenly concerned about the receivables.

"You need special attention," he said. "We're going to put you in our workout group."

"What's that?"

His answer sounded evasive.

"They help you work out your problems. The guy you need to see is in the second story of our location over on Lake Street. As soon as you get this issue resolved, you can come back to us for your banking needs."

This seemed odd. I consulted my friend and CPA Bill Patty.

"You need an attorney," he said.

Bill connected me with Mike McEllistrem, a young, athletic, and very bright lawyer who could compete with Gordy Bourne, the ex-Marine at UNIVAC, with his choice of words.

When I told Mike about my problem with First National Bank, adding that I saw the issue as temporary, he said, "John, if they put you in the workout group, they want your ass out of the bank."

"That's not what they told me."

"I used to work in the workout group at First Bank," he said. "I know what I'm talking about."

Together, we visited Time Management Corporation, where Mike pulled out a yellow notepad. "John has this list of what you owe him," he told a manager. "Do you see a problem with this list?"

"No."

"How is he doing on deliveries?"

"Doing good."

"How about the product quality?"

"We really like it."

"Do you plan to pay him?"

"Yes."

"Can you give us a schedule?"

"Yes."

Two days later, schedule in hand, I went and introduced myself to the First National workout banker, upstairs in the small branch on Lake Street.

"John! Good to see you."

"Yeah," I said. "It's kind of new for me to be in something called a workout group."

As we started talking and I showed him my documentation and the Time Management payment plan, I learned that the young man was a fellow North Dakotan. So, we had more things to talk about. "This sounds good," he said after reviewing my material. "You're working through the issue."

Before long, TMC was back in regular banking. Only then did I learn that it is rare for entrepreneurs to make it out of a workout group successfully. Dave Peterson at First National Bank in St. Paul continued working with us, and eventually, we had a working line of two to three million dollars.

As for our move to Dunseith, which is where my banking saga started—it was a good decision. Our workers from Belcourt, most of whom stayed with us, traveled in a TMC-organized van pool from the reservation to the new location—and there was plenty of room to grow.

Addition by addition, we took the city-owned building up to fifty thousand square feet. In some cases, federal grants for an expansion were made available to the city that varied in size, depending on the number of new jobs we were going to create.

The grants were awarded on a competitive basis. But the city had to apply for them, and I and a city council member had to travel to the EDA regional office in Denver to present a case to them. After our second successful pitch, they laughed when we came to see them again. "How much do you want this time?"

In other cases, we received government-guaranteed loans for facilities or equipment. To my surprise, the US Department of Housing and Urban Development later presented Bob and me with a recognition for paying a loan back in full. Apparently, not everyone pays off a government loan.

Eventually, TMC invested in building additional space. By the time we sold the company, the plant had grown to one hundred thousand square feet, half of which was city-owned. We had 350 employees and were shipping $1 million in product most weeks.

Part E:

Retirement

25.

Finding a Buyer

I WAS APPROACHING sixty-five and enjoying our success and the work with my team more than ever when the final agenda item in our semiannual board of directors meeting brought a surprise. "Is there any other business?" I said, about to adjourn.

My CPA friend and board member Bill Patty spoke up. "We should sell the company."

"But—I don't understand this," I said. "I love what I do."

"Our earnings are good," Bill continued, "and the multiples that establish the selling price are high."

The meeting had shown that the directors were pleased with the company's performance, and Bill hadn't told me he was going to broach the topic. Scanning the room to gauge people's reactions, I saw that most of the other board members looked equally surprised.

Finally, one of them, Roger Durkee, said, "John, what happens if you wake up one morning and you can't do what you like doing?"

MY MAIN CONCERN during the selling process was to ensure the future of the company and its workers. This meant avoiding investor-type buyers who knew nothing about manufacturing in the high-tech sector and would just dump TMC at the next opportunity.

When Bill suggested selling TMC, Pat and I reached out to a young mergers and acquisitions expert, Lindi Doherty, who had impressed us when we met her at a conference hosted by her then-employer, an investment bank headquartered in Minneapolis, Piper Jaffray and Co. Lindi was now working independently. Between her as our sell-side consultant and our attorney, Mike McEllistrem, we ended up with a powerful team.

From Lindi, I learned how important it is not to get distracted during the selling process and to keep running the business smoothly.

"A lot can go wrong during a company sale and due diligence processes," she said, "and if the eye is taken off the ball, then the company might be worth less going forward. You also don't want your employees leaving because they think the company is going to be sold."

After preparing a TMC sale/marketing memorandum, Lindi put out feelers to identify potential buyers. Initial leads were located on the West Coast and in Florida and included an owner of nursing homes whom I visited but didn't seriously consider. Then an electronics manufacturer in Rochester, Minnesota, that had spun off from IBM emerged as an interested strategic buyer: Pemstar.

Founded in 1994, the company had facilities in Europe, Asia, and Mexico, with fast-growing revenue—from $7 million in their first year to $32 million in 1997 and $165 million in 1998. The CEO, Al Berning, was already a star in the industry. In 1999, he was named the National Ernst & Young Emerging Entrepreneur of the Year.

I liked the Pemstar idea—but I did have a problem with their interpretation of confidentiality. A day or two after Lindi sent them our sales package, which described TMC's operations and provided detailed, confidential financial and customer information, I received a call from an IBM purchasing agent in Rochester.

"I understand your company is for sale."

"Really? Where did you get that?"

Lindi called Berning. "We had a confidentiality agreement. Send that whole damn package back!"

They did—and then they started pleading with us to reconsider.

By June 20, 2000, we had an agreement in place for Pemstar to acquire TMC. Six weeks later, on August 1, the acquisition was completed at an aggregate purchase price for the company's shares of more than $18 million. With its acquisition of TMC, Pemstar gained one hundred thousand square feet of factory space, technologically advanced manufacturing and test equipment, a trained and proven workforce that included a strong engineering staff, and an established and high-quality customer base.

The following week, Berning took Pemstar public on NASDAQ, with shares totaling $92.4 million.

26.

Giving Back

I CONTINUED TO MANAGE TMC, which was now a wholly owned subsidiary of Pemstar, as president of the company, until 2005. One of my favorite memories from that time is a customer appreciation day that we organized in 2002. The purchasing agents from Honeywell, 3M, IBM, and a few smaller companies were there, as were then-Governor John Hoeven and other local politicians, and, of course, Pat, Mike, Bob, the management team, and all our employees. Essentially, the event brought together the two groups of people that had made us successful: our customers, who provided opportunity, and our employees, who worked hard to satisfy our customers' needs.

The party also showed our diversity. TMC was a melting pot where Native Americans and people with German, Scandinavian, and Anglo-Saxon backgrounds worked side by side. I felt good about this; in a way, it reminded me of my childhood in Underwood, where half our neighbors' last names ended in *-son*, indicating Northern European ancestry.

The day after the party, I made good on a promise that I had given two IBM engineers who were New Yorkers, Sergio Rodriguez and Joe Gianatassio. We went on a "Lewis and Clark expedition."

Aware that Sergio was well traveled and had returned only recently from a trip to Japan, I tried my best to exceed expectations and introduce the two New Yorkers to the beauty of North Dakota, a rural state in what some call fly-over country.

On our list of stops were Rugby, the geographical center of North America; underground silos housing an intercontinental ballistic missile; and the Lewis and Clark Interpretive Center and replica of Fort Mandan overlooking the Missouri River near Washburn, where the two explorers spent the winter.

We saw the Garrison Dam, where I worked on a survey crew for two summers; visited Underwood, which, by then, had lost much of its vibrancy; enjoyed grilled sandwiches and extra-thick malts at Evander's pharmacy, now called Sodas and Things; and continued through the Bakken oil patch that brought us energy independence and westward to Medora.

Best known for musical performances held in the 2,800-seat Burning Hills Amphitheater during the summer, Medora is located at the gateway to the Teddy Roosevelt National Park and is the kind of place where bartenders hand out flyswatters. To this day, I wish I had a picture of the two New Yorkers and me sitting in the Iron Horse bar, insect deterrent in one hand and a beer in the other, as mile-long coal trains rushed by, causing the whole building to shake.

While our show that evening closed early because of rain, Sergio and Joe got a good sense of life in my home state. As we were enjoying a preperformance pitchfork steak fondue—yes, that's prime beef on pitchforks cooked in a barrel of hot oil—and taking in the view of the North Dakota Badlands, I spotted the dean of the NDSU pharmacy school at the next table. Soon afterward, I found myself talking with two strangers sitting across from us who had come from Minot—and learned that we had friends in common.

When you're from a small state like North Dakota, it seems people are always connected in some way, even if they're from different towns. For a New Yorker like Sergio, this was an alien experience. "Do you know everyone?" he said.

A few years later, he called me from his house in New York. "I've been to many places," he said. "But the visit to North Dakota with Medora and the Lewis and Clark tour—what a memorable trip!"

AS I VISITED Underwood in the early 2000s with Sergio and on a few other occasions, it pained me to see how much it had changed. What I remembered as a town filled with postwar energy and optimism now felt empty and lifeless.

By this time, I no longer had family in Underwood. Mom died from cancer in 1977; she was sixty-nine. Dad, who was fourteen years older, died in 1984, at ninety-one. My sister Colleen had moved to Washington State, Sonja to Florida.

Sonja, Colleen, Mom, Dad, and I in our living room, circa 1977.

But my memories were alive as ever—and I felt gratitude toward the community for putting me and others of my generation on a path to success. Many of my friends had gone on to get their college degrees, quite a few with PhDs, and others had excelled in special trades, including pipefitting and construction management. Now, I felt, it was time to give back.

Recalling the outstanding education that I had received in my hometown, I became active in the Underwood School Foundation. Together with some of the locals, I cofounded a real-estate investment company, Underwood Commercial Properties, Inc., to rejuvenate the main street. Our plan was to purchase closed downtown buildings and upgrade them for easy lease to potential business owners.

In the process, I talked to a former Underwood mayor-turned-state-legislator, Claudia Ash Tauer-Stromberg, who said, "Underwood has changed, Tip. You should maybe reconsider before investing there." I thought, *Well, maybe I can change it back a bit.*

We bought one building and turned it into a seven-room hotel and converted another to a much-needed good restaurant. Shag Mac Phee's daughter Pam told me recently about a family reunion that they celebrated in Underwood. "We booked every room in the hotel," she said.

With small towns suffering across the country, I am glad that I got involved in Underwood as I did. That said, if one's sole intention is to earn a return, most investments should come from the brain, not from the heart. Both the hotel and the restaurant are still open, but I eventually returned my stock in the real-estate company to the treasurer at no cost, with the hope that the local shareholders will continue their attempts to keep our hometown going.

As recently as 2021, the outlook was bleak. The major employer in the area, a coal-fired power plant owned by a utility provider in Minnesota with an adjacent lignite coal mine to fuel the plant, was facing closure because of Minnesota's green-energy mandates. In 2022, the plant luckily sold to North Dakota-based Rainbow Energy Center, and the new owners will continue the operation and add carbon capture and storage equipment. Innovation over regulation? Works for me.

Overall, Claudia was right about the changes in my hometown. Much of the land is now owned by families who have acquired adjacent acreage or are farming under contract for absentee owners. The small farms and family-owned shops that provided for homesteaders from Europe and their children and grandchildren have been replaced by much bigger enterprises. Thanks to changes in technology that have brought us big tractors, combines, and seeders, farmers can now work the land faster and more efficiently with almost no hired hands. But few kids grow up living on farms and working there, and the country schools have disappeared. Not all progress is good.

It's been a while since my last visit to Underwood, but I hope to go back for what might be a last time. While many of the people who shaped my experience as a young man, from my folks to Mel Koenig, Percy Evander, John Torske, and Shag Mac Phee have passed on and others, like Johnny Busch, have long left town, I want to see the few remaining old friends and the new headstone now marking Ernie's and Sophie's graves.

After I sold TMC, I probably had more money than I anticipated. Happy to support aspiring entrepreneurs, I invested in a couple of start-ups. One of the proposals was a mattress factory presented by David Bjorkman, a son of Pat's sister. He and his partner needed funds to get the project going. We agreed that I would purchase stock in their corporation that they would buy back from me at twice the price. The enterprise did well, but when they wanted to open another store in a neighboring state immediately following the start-up phase, I thought this plan was premature. I objected to the idea, and they purchased all my stock at the agreement price.

My other investment was in a health-care facility in the Moorhead-Fargo area, Lilac Homes, which offers assisted living and memory care for residents with dementia. It was the idea of Pat's nephew Bill Nelson and his wife, Gina, a nurse.

Bill had been successful as a manager for UPS when he called me and asked to meet one day as I was on my way home from Dunseith. At the Dairy Queen in Barnesville, he laid out his plan for Lilac Homes.

"I got everything lined up," he said. "Except—the bank needs just a little more money to get us over the hump."

I liked Bill and Gina's idea, his plan, and the presentation. Feeling convinced that they would be successful, I made a small investment to get things started for them. When they made the last payment on the note with me, they picked up food and stopped by for a little celebration. Earlier this year, right before Russia's invasion of Ukraine, they made the news in local and regional media after arranging a flight to safety in Minnesota for a young Ukrainian family. As I read and watched the reporting, I felt proud of them and grateful to have been a part of their story.

My investments in the mattress factory and Lilac Homes remind me of the UDAG grant that the City of Dunseith received before TMC's relocation. The city did not have funds for the upgrades that we needed, so the UDAG got them "over the hump" for our move there to grow the business. I think most investors learn that not all projects turn out to be successful, but we need not mention those experiences.

IN JANUARY 2005, I retired from TMC. "Dear Friends," I wrote in an email to my contacts at 3M, IBM, Honeywell, and other companies, "I want to extend to each of you the best of everything during the coming year. I also want to thank you for the opportunity you have extended to Turtle Mountain Corporation and Pemstar through the years. You have all been to the plant in Dunseith and seen the dramatic impact that the work you have sent there has had on the local community and employees. I'm sure that I speak for all of the employees when I extend our appreciation."

After sharing that Pat and I would be in Florida for the rest of the winter and expressing an open invitation for people to join us for a good game of golf in Fort Myers, I wrote, "I don't know what my expectations were when Bob and I started the company in 1974, but they surely were exceeded. The performance of our employees and the opportunity to meet and work with so many fine people, our customers, and suppliers, brought me extreme satisfaction. I'm sure the Dunseith team will continue to do a very good job meeting your needs in the future."

Over the course of the next few days, well-wishes and comments on the work these people and TMC had done together flooded my inbox. Pat Wheeler from 3M highlighted "the accomplishment of building such a strong, trusted, and enduring company." Mike Neumar from IBM wrote, "Your honesty and integrity are benchmarks for others to try to achieve." Norman Koning from 3M said that our contributions to the 3M Library Systems business "will long be remembered."

27.

Late Lessons and an Outlook

AS IT TURNED OUT, the Pemstar people learned too late how to run a business the bootstrap way and to adjust the overhead costs to compete in the contract manufacturing business. They had a great team of talented people, but, like Atron, they lacked a strategy for long-term success. And slogans like "You are not a player in the business until you reach a billion in revenue" may sound good, but a focus on the top line with little concern for bottom-line earnings is often a recipe for disaster. And so, the debt kept piling up.

I remember attending a management meeting before I retired, in which the Pemstar people said, "We're changing banks because the new one is giving us a better rate. It better fits our needs."

I didn't have a vote, but as the president of a wholly owned subsidiary of Pemstar, I was required by the bank to sign off on new loan agreements. And I could voice my opinion. I said, "You're talking about borrowing all this money. What's the plan for paying it back?"

Deadly silence.

In January 2007, Pemstar was sold to Benchmark Electronics, which was then headquartered in Angleton, Texas, and moved to Tempe, Arizona, ten years later. Benchmark's overhead rates were right in line with TMC's, but in 2015 they closed the Dunseith location, leaving the one-hundred-thousand-square-foot facility empty and putting many people out of work. It was a sad day for the Turtle Mountain region and a sad day for me.

The way I see it, Benchmark was geographically too far removed from the northern end of North Dakota, and cultural differences may have played a role, too. But I also have to wonder about my own contribution to TMC's closure. Did I not do my due diligence when I went looking for a buyer? Back then, if anyone had asked me about my hopes or dreams, I would have said that I want the company to thrive in all perpetuity. Was I perhaps blinded by the enthusiastic headlines about Pemstar?

When the plant closed, someone kindly sent me a box containing objects of sentimental value, thereby rescuing it from destination dumpster. Rummaging through the container, I found some plaques that customers had given us in recognition of our excellent service level, like the IBM Quality Performance Award and the 3M Certified Supplier Award.

In the end, these big-company awards meant just as much or more to me than some other recognitions. I was surprised and grateful to receive the NDSU Alumni Achievement Award in 1996 and to be inducted into the North Dakota Entrepreneur Hall of Fame in 2004 for "long-standing entrepreneurial contributions to the state and nation." When TMC received the Small Business Administration Award for Excellence in 1986, I jumped on the opportunity to take Pat and our three children to Washington, DC, and visit the Tomb of the Unknown Soldier with them. But for an entrepreneur, it doesn't get much better than having a bunch of happy customers.

Following my retirement, Pat and I spent the winters in Florida. We focused on family and friends, played golf, went on cruises with friends, and visited China, France, and Ireland with college classmates. We continued to see Bill Patty and his wife, Missy, whom many people knew as a dog-loving bird bander. When Missy died in December 2021, the *St. Paul Pioneer Press* published a long obituary about The Bird Lady of North Oaks, a "lifelong advocate for the natural world."[39]

Pat always looked elegant.

As for some of the other people important to our success, Frank X. Morin died even before we sold TMC; Randy Erickson passed more recently, and his funeral was the last time I sang a solo in our church; Mike McEllistrem is a partner at Taft Stettinius & Hollister LLP in Minneapolis; and Hy Osofsky, who returned to UNIVAC after the MDS-Atron merger, lives in Arizona, and I have enjoyed catching up with him recently.

Bob was with TMC until 2004. He and I have stayed close and talk often. We were both excited to learn in April 2022 that the City of Dunseith found a buyer for the vacant TMC facility.

Hoefer Group was planning to turn it into a production site for ultralight RVs.

On other days, my conversations with Bob revolve around the work that we did together. One time, when he and I were reminiscing about TMC, he commended me for negotiating "a hell of a deal" and getting us going with $2,500 in cash and zero bank debt. We were a good team, and I was fortunate to have him as a business partner.

SOMEONE RECENTLY ASKED ME whether I feel any regrets about my professional or personal life. There's one thing, a lesson that has to do with procrastination: don't wait to talk about things. When Dad passed, I realized too late that I had missed the opportunity to ask him about his early years. What was it like to be in foster care in Sweden? And then to return to the United States alone, as a young man of seventeen who didn't speak English?

Two years ago, in January 2020, Pat passed away. She had been in and out of the hospital for a while, and I was used to her always coming back home. This time, two days before she died, I spent the first night with her, and our daughter Kristi stayed for the second night because I had appointments the following morning. One was to see a doctor and the other was at our house, where I had scheduled workers to install handrails alongside the steps leading from the house to the garage. Pat always had her hands full when coming to the car. Having a railing there felt important to me. I didn't want her to fall.

I know that I was there for Pat throughout her health problems, taking her to appointments and looking out for her. I also know that her faith was strong and believe that she must have felt guided by God on this final journey that she took. But I never asked her whether there was any unfinished business she might want to discuss, never invited her to share with me her thoughts during those last days and weeks. Did I do enough?

By the time I was done with my appointments, at around noon, Pat was barely communicative, and I could hardly talk to her. She died late that day, surrounded by our family, other close relatives, and Pastor Omland. We were married sixty-two years.

Among the notes that I received after Pat's passing was one from her niece in Montana, Liz McIntosh. Liz shared childhood memories of Pat taking her on shopping sprees and to the salon; of parties for weddings, birthdays, and anniversaries that Pat organized; and of her own wedding, where Pat brought tears to everyone's eyes when she and I sang "Sunrise, Sunset" from the musical *Fiddler on the Roof* as a duet. "Unforgettable!" her niece wrote.

The picture that Liz paints of Pat is one that most people who knew her would recognize: a generous, compassionate woman with a wonderful voice, who made everyone feel welcome.

One of the many things I miss about Pat is her subtle sense of humor. At her retirement party in 2002, which her assistant of seventeen years, Kim, helped organize, Pat recalled for the audience the early days of TMC, followed by a big shout-out to Kim. "John told me I needed to manage the money, of all things! Can you imagine his courage with my training as a home economics teacher and my spending habits?"

Then she described how she and Kim, a University of Minnesota accounting graduate and CPA, took charge of the company. "We told the guys, 'You go sell and ship product, and we'll take care of the money.' When there wasn't enough money, we told them they had better get after it."

WITH PAT GONE and the house quiet, I am involved in various projects, including at church and at NDSU, and stay connected to old friends. In calls with Merrill and Dody Johnson, who lived a few houses from us at our first Shoreview address, we reminisce about the time they nailed our garage door shut on

Halloween night and other pranks. My best man, Syl Melroe, and I also talk often, sharing memories and laughs about our time as students.

When I learned recently that NDSU wants to increase their diversity in the STEM departments, I thought how young men and women from the Turtle Mountain Band of Chippewa might feel more at home with other Catholic students and could room with them on campus, in the faith-based St. Paul's Newman Center. I have since then suggested to NDSU that they start recruiting Native American high school kids the way they recruit athletes. Many of these young men and women will be first-generation students, who might need extra support with their applications and scholarships. But I'm sure it can be done.

Our church, where Pat and I worshipped, served, and sang in the choir for forty-plus years, has some of the problems many other churches do: overall membership, service attendance, and giving are down.

I know this is a nationwide trend that, in part, is related to the restrictions of COVID-19. But here's the deal: the Great Commission calls us to spread the word and be inclusive. And given the impact that the church has had on my family and many of my friends, I cannot simply accept that it is irrelevant in today's society. Put differently, failure is not an option.

The way I see it, a church could be run like a business, with financial and membership goals established for the short and long terms, and with accountability to the congregation. Members need to be encouraged to use their talents in ministries and committees, ranging from maintenance and finance to worship and music. Like employees, all members must be made to feel that they matter and that their participation in the day-to-day life of the church will make the congregation stronger. The keyword is *synergy*. And then, of course, the pastoral care needs to remain apolitical and, in general, exceed all expectations.

AS I REFLECT on my life, with gratitude to have been part of creating a beautiful family and building a successful company, I am also cognizant of roads not taken, such as a military career. Commissioned in 1957, I had an eight-year obligation in the Army Reserve. In June 1965, having satisfied this obligation, I went down to the Army headquarters and asked for a resignation form. "Lieutenant Miller," they said, "we have your captain bars here. You should reconsider this." I held firm.

In some ways, my schedule was lucky. I was much too young for World War II, and by the time I started college, in the fall of 1953, the Korean War had ended. In the Vietnam War, ground troops weren't deployed until President Lyndon Johnson launched Operation Rolling Thunder in 1965, and the reserves weren't called up until 1967. By then, I was serving my country indirectly, as a mechanical engineer at UNIVAC working on projects for the Navy, and Pat and I had three kids.

Our children have fortunately stayed close. They live within a few miles, and I look forward every day to visits from them or one of our eight grandchildren. My daughters, Lisa and Kristi, stop by and prepare meals, and my son, Mike, and I spend three evenings a week together. He comes with food, and we watch movies and talk business and politics.

I will admit that I sometimes find it hard to understand the actions of our government. Our withdrawal from Afghanistan in 2021 was a debacle and a complete waste of our investment there, and our initial hesitation in Ukraine to adequately arm the country made us seem weak. Not to mention how the COVID-19 pandemic affected people's lives when children couldn't attend school because teachers unions wielded their power.

What worries me economically and militarily is the rise of China, a country that uses slave labor and steals our technology. We should stop sending our money and the manufacturing of everything, from pills to cars, over to a foreign country whose goal it is to overtake us. Our money finances their military! Maybe it's time to put the kibosh on outsourcing to unfriendly countries overseas and bring the work back home so that our young people will find the same opportunities that my generation found after World War II.

The environment that my grandsons and granddaughters are growing up in is very different from my own background. None of them joined the Scouts, but they all know how to swim and are even qualified for lifesaving. Growing up in the affluent suburbs of St. Paul, they have been sheltered from physical hardship, and while they are a good mix of excellent athletes and great students, few of them will leave high school or even college with much work experience. As they venture out to make a living and raise a family—I bet years later than Pat and I did—they will have to learn new skills simultaneously, like working with different bosses, keeping commitments, and money management. But, knowing them as I do, I have complete confidence and faith that they will be up to the task, probably with fewer problems than Pat and I faced, and they will exceed my expectations.

If any of them were to ask me about the path to successful entrepreneurship, I would tell them that the bootstrap way works if you're creative, ambitious, and willing to learn new things and persevere.

Say "we" more often than "I."

Protect the honesty and integrity of your name in everything you do.

And always remember your great-grandmother Sophie's words: "If you don't have time to say hello, you're too busy."

Thank you
for reading my memoir.

If you have a moment,
I would appreciate a review
on Amazon or Goodreads.

Twelve Suggestions for Success

1. No capital? Be creative!
What do Coca-Cola, Craigslist, and Microsoft have in common? All three companies were bootstrapped; their founders had an idea but no money or funding. This approach comes with slow growth and cash flow restrictions that can cause stress. On the upside are freedom from pressure by outside investors; more flexibility; opportunities for finding creative solutions and for learning to run a business with low overhead, low inventory, and an eye on the bottom line.
(Chapters 8, 12, 27)

2. Know yourself.
The better you know yourself when you start a business, the easier you will be able to deal with challenges. This means knowing your strengths, skills, and values, and being clear-eyed about your limitations so that you can plan for workarounds.
(Chapters 2–7, 13–16)

3. Experience matters.
While formal education is important—Earl Hanson would not have hired me if I did not have my BSME—work experience counts for a lot. There's nothing like a job for learning how to take responsibility, work with a team, supervise, lead, mentor, sell, make a budget, and stick to it.
(Chapters 2–6, 11, 14–16)

4. Know your why.
Why do you want to own and run a business? Why do you want to make your organization successful? Especially in the early years, having a solid answer to these questions will help you

weather the ups and downs of being an entrepreneur and leader. And having a purpose beyond profit will help motivate you and everyone around you.
(Chapters 1, 7, 9, 17, 26)

5. Build the right team.
Statistics show that companies established as a partnership of two or more people are more successful than solo ventures. If possible, try to find a business partner who complements your strengths and weaknesses. Having someone on your board, or as an adviser, who will be honest about necessary changes and adjustments is essential—provided you can listen. Other key people include your attorney, CPA, and a banker.
(Chapters 10, 16, 21, 24)

6. Take the time to say hello.
Say hello, start a conversation, and you may be surprised what can happen. You might discover that you share friends or acquaintances, went to the same college or university, have the same interests. From there, opportunities arise to find a new market, customer, or employee. Not to mention that saying hello makes life more pleasant.
(Chapters 20, 25–27)

7. Create synergy and show your appreciation.
Call it *workforce engagement*, call it *synergy*: the idea behind the term is that the whole is greater than the sum of its parts. Getting everyone in a company pulling in the same direction increases productivity and customer satisfaction and keeps employees happy. Showing appreciation for everyone's contributions to the success of your organization goes a long way. This gets me back to my last point: take the time to say hello.
(Chapters 17–18)

8. Stick to your knitting and keep an open mind.

Especially during the start-up phase, where you're working on earning your customers' trust, it is important to set boundaries for which kind of services your company provides. By doing so, you will help maintain a high service level. As your company grows, you want to keep an open mind for opportunities leading to diversification.
(Chapter 19)

9. Quality equals profit.

By focusing on quality, you are making customer satisfaction your top priority. This leads to repeat business and referrals. It also helps reduce the number of errors, which means you're not redoing work, and, in turn, saving money. By documenting your mistakes and establishing processes to avoid them, you can ensure continuous improvement.
(Chapter 22)

10. Listen to your customers.

Listening to your customers means learning about their needs and hearing their complaints. Their needs will lead you to your product-market fit. If they have bad things to say about your service level, product, or employees, don't be defensive. Instead, try to get as much information out of them as possible: "Can you tell me more?"
(Chapter 17)

11. Be honest.

Even before a customer starts working with you, they're evaluating whether they can trust you: Is this person "baffling with bullshit or dazzling with brilliance"? First impressions count for a lot, and your being honest and authentic in your interactions with them will help answer their question. Once a relationship has been established, be honest about any mistakes that your

company made: "We screwed up. We'll fix it." Equally important: if you say you will do something, it is important to keep
that commitment or request a change.
(Chapters 6, 17, 23–24)

12. Don't give up.

As an entrepreneur, you will face setbacks, so don't get too comfortable and forget about the bad times when things are going
well. And if your company does hit a low point, remember that
there is a fine line between perseverance and stupidity: You will
want to assess honestly whether your business has a future. If the
answer is yes, don't give up. Try to learn from adversity and see
it as a growth opportunity.
(Chapters 12–13)

Coauthor's Afterword

John and I had just completed the second draft of his manuscript when he called me with a suggestion. "I think you should see North Dakota," he said. "It might be an interesting experience." A few weeks later, we were on the road together, accompanied by his son, Mike, and my husband, Martin.

"How was it in North Dakota?" friends in California asked me after our return home, their tone betraying a curiosity often reserved for exotic destinations. "It was great," I said. Then, I told them about wide, empty landscapes—North Dakota is fourteen times the size of my Austrian home state, Tyrol, but no more populous—and about handshakes that feel as solid as they used to in the Tyrol before the takeover of the hug.

I told them about John, whom I knew from dozens of phone calls but didn't meet face-to-face until he and Mike picked us up from the airport in Bismarck. Our three days together confirmed previous impressions. John cares deeply about North Dakota and his hometown, Underwood. He thrives in group settings, and his mindset is generous. When introducing me to others, he would cover the same bullet points—journalist, Austria, Los Angeles—and sometimes add a caveat. "We don't agree politically. But that doesn't matter."

I described to my friends a brunch at JD's Garage, the renamed restaurant that John's group of investors created in Underwood, where friends and neighbors swapped stories about the Miller family and spoke candidly about the challenges facing their hometown, and meetings in Dunseith, where former employees, city officials, and business owners talked with excitement about their experience with TMC. I shared with them how touching it felt to spend time with a 99-year-old World War II veteran in Underwood, Howard Busch, whom I thanked for liberating Europe from the Nazis, and recounted a visit with Governor Doug Burgum in the state capitol in Bismarck. Wearing blue jeans and boots, he introduced himself with "I'm Doug." He spent half an hour with us, listening intently as John told him about TMC and showed him a core memory board that was built on the Turtle Mountain Reservation.

Our group of four covered eight hundred miles in three days, with the Underwood Inn serving as basecamp. We saw the Garrison Dam and Lake Sakakawea, which is forty miles longer than the Tyrol. We drove past grain elevators, draglines, oil pumps, and windmills that speak to the status of agriculture and energy as the state's largest industrial sectors. We enjoyed a patriotic performance and a pitchfork steak fondue at the Medora Musical, with the canyons of the Badlands across from the arena creating a backdrop of sheer rock, grass, and trees that is vast and rugged and commands the same respect as landscapes in the American Southwest. On our last day, Bob Wilmot took us on a quick tour of the Turtle Mountains, a long stretch of rolling hills created during the last ice age, and shared with us vistas of the prairie reaching to the southern horizon.

Bob, who is from Jamestown and now lives in Rugby, was one of many North Dakotans welcoming us with open arms. Calm and reserved, he drove us around Dunseith, where two-thirds of the population is Native American. "It is all very well integrated," he said, adding that authorities like the Sheriff's office and the Bureau of Indian Affairs work hand in hand.

Later, he shared with me the feeling of satisfaction that he used to derive from his work. "At the end of the week, I would look at the truck loaded up with high-tech products ready to go to our customers and think what an accomplishment!" He remembers staying optimistic about TMC's success, even as the company hit bottom in 1977. "I always thought that we would somehow survive," he said.

Only twenty-two when John hired him to manage the newly created plant, Bob had good instincts for effective leadership and tried to spend as much time as possible on the factory floor engaging with workers. "My philosophy is to be seen when all is well, and people will talk to you if something goes wrong," he said.

For a lunch at Dale's Truck Stop in Dunseith, Bob brought together a motley group of TMC fans. The restaurant owner, George Gottbreht, a former mayor of Dunseith, Bob Leonhard, and a local grocery store owner, Wayne Barbot, talked about the company's contribution to the larger community and reminisced about the annual corn feed and the gifts of turkey at Thanksgiving. "One year, they needed 360 birds," Wayne said. "When I called my suppliers with the order, they thought I'd been drinking."

Former employees, many of them Native American, sounded emotional as they reflected on their experience working at TMC. Terry Gladue said, "It was like a family." Loyal to the company and its successors for twenty-one years, until Benchmark pulled out of Dunseith in 2015, she recalled the day everyone learned about the plant closure. "They informed us at a big company meeting in February," she said. "We thought it was going to be about our bonuses. But then—your heart just fell." Bill Tuttle, who was in the engineering group, said that working for John and Bob was "the gold standard." And Denny Bonn, who was on the maintenance crew, later spoke of his twenty-eight years at TMC as "the best job I had in my whole life."

In the voices of these men and women, I heard sadness for the loss they experienced and pride for the high-tech work they used to do. "We were all so dedicated," Georgie Gladue recalled. "I knew nothing about soldering. But I did a good job the first time." She spent thirty-two years at TMC, ending her career as a foreman.

The hope at the time of our visit was that the new plant owners, Charles Hoefer and his wife, Andrea Kine, would pick up with their RV manufacturing business where things stopped seven years earlier. Having learned from Burgum's office about the vacant factory, they were able to finance a remodel with support from the state government.

On a tour of the plant, Charles, who is from Indiana, spoke respectfully of "the history in the walls of the building." He sounded excited about a new career and technology center under construction in Dunseith where high school students will be able to receive college-level certification as RV technicians, as well as in other areas. "The training program will create a feeder system for our plant," he said.

After our return to L.A., somebody asked me whether anything surprised me on our trip. Yes, what struck me about North Dakotans is their relentless commitment to community.

At the Sunday brunch in Underwood, where members of the Anderson, Arndt, Cottingham, Haseleu, LeRoy, Paulson, Rasmusson, and Schell families gathered to reconnect with John, most agreed that the town's future looked uncertain at best. Terri Wolf, who keeps Sodas and Things going, later summed up people's feelings. "It's kind of scary," she said. "We're lucky that the mine and the powerplant didn't shut down."

Underwood, which used to be prosperous enough to support three car dealerships, has become a victim of twentieth-century progress that brought increased mobility and a population shift toward cities. While Sodas and Things still serve malts and grilled cheese sandwiches to guests propped on vinyl-covered bar stools, prescriptions picked up there are filled at a pharmacy in Turtle Lake. Von's Clothing, where Mike remembers shopping for jeans with his grandmother Sophie, is long gone. The main street feels empty. And the only grocery store, a Dollar General, sits out on a four-lane highway, US 83.

But the spirit of community that John remembers so well is still palpable. I saw it at the brunch, where Susan Cottingham and other guests volunteered to help in the understaffed kitchen. I heard it in the words of a younger resident, Amanda Haseleu, who thanked John for initiating infrastructure investments. "You brought excitement to this town," she said. And I saw it again in Susan's sister, Diane Schell, who runs the Underwood Inn. Her dedication and high standards show a deep connection to her roots. Like so many in Underwood, she is determined to keep her small town alive. Failure, as John would say, is not an option.

John Miller with Governor Doug Burgum in the North Dakota state capitol.
(Photo courtesy of Governor Burgum's office. July 2022.)

Acknowledgments

Writing and publishing *Bootstrap Entrepreneur* sometimes reminded me of building and running a company: it was a collaborative task.

Mike Miller, my son, keeps my computer running.

Hy Osofsky, my former colleague and friend at UNIVAC and Atron, generously shared his experience as a logic design engineer in the pioneering days of computer technology.

Lindi Doherty, who was instrumental in the sale of TMC, freely shared her expertise and her memories of the process.

Dawn Seay from the office of Governor Doug Burgum (North Dakota) helped verify the accuracy of a story about him that is included in this book.

Josh Schwartz, founder of Pubvendo, helped me get the word out.

My coauthor, Christina Schweighofer, and her team of editors, proofreaders, and graphic designers made writing and producing this book a rewarding adventure. Her husband, Martin Leitner, advised me on marketing options.

I feel grateful to everyone listed above for their help. And I am thankful for the many people who shaped my journey as a person and as an entrepreneur by providing a lifetime of guidance, support, hard work, and love. While some of them are mentioned by name in this book, many others are not because of space restrictions. This does not in any way lessen their contribution.

Notes

1. David Boslaugh, "First-Hand: No Damned Computer Is Going to Tell Me What to Do: The Story of the Naval Tactical Data System, NTDS," Engineering and Technology Wiki, last modified May 12, 2021, https://ethw.org/First-Hand:No_Damned_Computer_is_Going_to_Tell_Me_What_to_DO_-_The_Story_of_the_Naval_Tactical_Data_System,_NTDS.

2. Boslaugh, "First-Hand."

3. J. A. N. Lee, *Computer Pioneers* (Los Alamitos: IEEE Computer Society Press, 1995), https://history.computer.org/pioneers/parker-je.html.

4. Tom Webb, "How St. Paul Was Almost Silicon Valley," *Twin Cities Pioneer Press*, January 2, 2010, https://www.twincities.com/2010/01/02/how-st-paul-was-almost-silicon-valley/.

5. William Moye, "ENIAC: The Army-Sponsored Revolution," The US Army Research Lab, https://ftp.arl.army.mil/~mike/comphist/96summary/.

6. J. A. N. Lee, *Computer Pioneers* (Los Alamitos: IEEE Computer Society Press, 1995), https://history.computer.org/pioneers/parker-je.html; Arthur Norberg, *Computers and Commerce: A Study of Technology and Management at Eckert-Mauchly Computer Company, Engineering Research Associates, and Remington Rand, 1946–1957* (Cambridge: The MIT Press, 2005), 82.

7. Simson Garfinkel and Rachel Grunspan, *The Computer Book: From the Abacus to Artificial Intelligence, 250 Milestones in the History of Computer Science* (New York: Sterling Publishing, 2018), "1972 Cray Research," Kindle.

8. David Lundstrom, *A Few Good Men from Univac* (Cambridge: The MIT Press, 1990), 53, https://tcm.computerhistory.org/exhibits/FewGoodMen.pdf.

9. Richard Margolis, "A Long List of Grievances," *New York Times*, November 12, 1972, https://nyti.ms/3P8MK96.

10. North Dakota Department of Public Instruction, "The History and Culture of the Turtle Mountain Band of Chippewa," 11, https://www.ndsu.edu/fileadmin/centers/americanindianhealth/files/History_and_Culture_Turtle_Mountain.pdf.

11. North Dakota Department of Public Instruction, "The History and Culture," 17.

12. State Historical Society of North Dakota, "Culture—Turtle Mountain," North Dakota Studies, https://www.ndstudies.gov/curriculum/high school/turtle-mountain/culture-turtle-mountain.

13. "A Tiny North Dakota Community," *NDSU Bison Briefs*, Winter 1991, 20.

14. David Billington, Donald Jackson, and Martin Melosi, *The History of Large Federal Dams: Planning, Design, and Construction*, (Denver: US Department of the Interior, 2005), 235, https://www.usbr.gov/history/HistoryofLargeDams/LargeFederalDams.pdf.

15. Billington, Jackson, and Melosi, *The History of Large Federal Dams*, 269–275.

16. Lisa Jones, "Three Tribes, a Dam and a Diabetes Epidemic," *High Country News*, May 23, 2011, https://www.hcn.org/issues/43.8/three-tribes-a-dam-and-a-diabetes-epidemic.

17. Brenda Shelkey, "On the Wings of a Prayer," *Underwood News* (Underwood, ND), November 12, 2009.

18. David Billington, Donald Jackson, and Martin Melosi, *The History of Large Federal Dams: Planning, Design, and Construction*, (Denver: U.S. Department of the Interior, 2005), 284, https://www.usbr.gov/history/HistoryofLargeDams/LargeFederalDams.pdf.

19. Dwight D. Eisenhower, "Address at the Closure Ceremony at Garrison Dam, North Dakota," June 11, 1953, transcript, https://www.presidency.ucsb.edu/documents/address-the-closure-ceremonies-garrison-dam-north-dakota.

20. Eisenhower, "Address at the Closure Ceremony."

21. Dilys Winegrad and Atsushi Akera, "A Short History of the Second American Revolution," *University of Pennsylvania Almanac*, January 30, 1996, https://almanac.upenn.edu/archive/v42/n18/eniac.html.

22. Simson Garfinkel and Rachel Grunspan, *The Computer Book: From the Abacus to Artificial Intelligence, 250 Milestones in the History of Computer Science* (New York: Sterling Publishing, 2018), "1964 IBM System/360," Kindle.

23. Clark Schenkenberger, "The Pants Tell the Story," *Spectrum* (Fargo, ND), November 2, 1956, 1.

24. Schenkenberger, "The Pants," 1.

25. "A Touch of the Match and Away We Go," *Spectrum*, 6.

26. Fred Hultz, "The President Speaks to the Student Body," *Spectrum*, 2.

27. Ed Mannion, letter to the editor, *Spectrum*, 2.

28. Lowell Benson, ed., "50 Years of Ocean Surveillance: An Information Technology Legacy Paper," VIP Club, NAWC/NADC Warminster Historical Information, August 2013, 2, https://www.navairdevcen.org/PDF/OceanSurveillance.pdf.

29. David Boslaugh, "First-Hand: No Damned Computer Is Going to Tell Me What to Do: The Story of the Naval Tactical Data System, NTDS," Engineering and Technology Wiki, last modified May 12, 2021, https://ethw.org/First-Hand:No_Damned_Computer_is_Going_to_Tell_Me_What_to_DO_-_The_Story_of_the_Naval_Tactical_Data_System,_NTDS.

30. Lloyd Dobbins and Clare Crawford-Mason, *Quality or Else: The Revolution in World Business* (New York: Houghton Mifflin Company, 1991), 256.

31. Dobbins and Crawford-Mason, *Quality or Else*, 1.

32. Homer Sarasohn, "First-Hand: Establishing Radio Communications in Post-WWII Japan," Engineering and Technology Wiki, excerpted and adapted from "Japanese Students Have Surpassed U.S. Teachers," by Bart Ziegler, Associated Press, *Greenwich Times*, April 23, 1990, https://ethw.org/First-Hand:Establishing_Radio_Communications_in_Post-WWII_Japan.

33. Sarasohn, "First-Hand."

34. Lloyd Dobbins and Clare Crawford-Mason, *Quality or Else: The Revolution in World Business* (New York: Houghton Mifflin Company, 1991), 13.

35. Dobbins and Crawford-Mason, *Quality or Else*, 14.

36. Homer Sarasohn, "First-Hand: Establishing Radio Communications in Post-WWII Japan," Engineering and Technology Wiki, excerpted and adapted from "Japanese Students Have Surpassed U.S. Teachers," by Bart Ziegler, Associated Press, *Greenwich Times*, April 23, 1990, https://ethw.org/First-Hand:Establishing_Radio_Communications_in_Post-WWII_Japan.

37. "About W E Deming," Deming Alliance, article courtesy of Alan Clark, https://demingalliance.org/about/w-e-deming/.

38. Dawn Bailey, "When Something Needed to Be Done About National Competitiveness...," National Institute of Standards and Technology, US Department of Commerce, August 16, 2018,

https://www.nist.gov/blogs/blogrige/when-something-needed-be-done-about-national-competitiveness.

39. Molly Guthrey, "Missy Patty, The Bird Lady of North Oaks, Dies at Age 88," *Twin Cities Pioneer Press*, December 17, 2021, https://www.twincities.com/2021/12/17/missy-patty-the-bird-lady-of-north-oaks-dies-at-age-88/.

Bibliography

"About W E Deming." Deming Alliance. Article courtesy of Alan Clark.
    https://demingalliance.org/about/w-e-deming/.
"A Tiny North Dakota Community." *NDSU Bison Briefs*, Winter 1991.
Bailey, Dawn. "When Something Needed to Be Done About National
    Competitiveness..." National Institute of Standards and Technology.
    U.S. Department of Commerce. August 16, 2018.
    https://www.nist.gov/blogs/blogrige/when-something-needed-be-done-
    about-national-competitiveness.
Benson, Lowell, ed. "50 Years of Ocean Surveillance: An Information
    Technology Legacy Paper." VIP Club. NAWC/NADC Warminster
    Historical Information. August 2013.
    https://www.navairdevcen.org/PDF/OceanSurveillance.pdf.
Billington, David, Donald Jackson, and Martin Melosi. *The History of Large
    Federal Dams: Planning, Design, and Construction.* Denver: U.S.
    Department of the Interior, 2005.
    https://www.usbr.gov/history/HistoryofLargeDams/
    LargeFederalDams.pdf.
Boslaugh, David. "First-hand: No Damned Computer Is Going to Tell Me
    What to Do: The Story of the Naval Tactical Data System, NTDS."
    Engineering and Technology Wiki. Last modified May 12, 2021.
    https://ethw.org/First-Hand:No_Damned_Computer_is_Going_
    to_Tell_Me_What_to_DO_-_The_Story_of_
    the_Naval_Tactical_Data_System,_NTDS.
Dobbins, Lloyd, and Clare Crawford-Mason. *Quality or Else: The Revolution
    in World Business.* New York: Houghton Mifflin Company, 1991.
Eisenhower, Dwight. "Address at the Closure Ceremony at Garrison Dam,
    North Dakota." June 11, 1953. Transcript.
    https://www.presidency.ucsb.edu/documents/address-the-closure-
    ceremonies-garrison-dam-north-dakota.
Fandrick, Ron, ed. *Underwood On-Line.* Last modified January 27, 2021.
    https://www.rwf2000.com/MainWindow.htm.
Forum. Fargo, ND. October 28,1956.
Garfinkel, Simson and Rachel Grunspan. *The Computer Book: From the
    Abacus to Artificial Intelligence, 250 Milestones in the History of Computer
    Science.* New York: Sterling Publishing, 2018.
Guthrey, Molly. "Missy Patty, The Bird Lady of North Oaks, Dies at Age 88."
    Twin Cities Pioneer Press, December 17, 2021.

https://www.twincities.com/2021/12/17/missy-patty-the-bird-lady-of-north-oaks-dies-at-age-88/.

Jones, Lisa. "Three Tribes, a Dam and a Diabetes Epidemic." *High Country News*, May 23, 2011. https://www.hcn.org/issues/43.8/three-tribes-a-dam-and-a-diabetes-epidemic.

Lee, J. A. N. *Computer Pioneers*. Los Alamitos: IEEE Computer Society Press, 1995.

Lukoff, Herman. *From Dits to Bits: A Personal History of the Electronic Computer*. Robotics. Cambridge: The MIT Press, 1979.

Lundstrom, David. *A Few Good Men from Univac*. Cambridge: The MIT Press, 1990.

Minot Daily News. "Garrison Dam Dedicated 60 Years Ago." June 28, 2013. https://www.minotdailynews.com/news/local-news/2013/06/garrison-dam-dedicated-60-years-ago/.

Moye, William. "ENIAC: The Army-Sponsored Revolution." The U.S. Army Research Lab. https://ftp.arl.army.mil/~mike/comphist/96summary/.

New York Times. "The Metaverse May Be Virtual But the Impact Will Be Real." November 12, 1972. https://www.nytimes.com/1972/11/12/archives/a-long-list-of-grievances-indians.html.

Norberg, Arthur. *Computers and Commerce: A Study of Technology and Management at Eckert-Mauchly Computer Company, Engineering Research Associates, and Remington Rand, 1946–1957*. Cambridge: The MIT Press, 2005.

North Dakota Department of Public Instruction. *The History and Culture of the Turtle Mountain Band of Chippewa*. Bismarck: North Dakota Department of Public Instruction, 1997. https://www.ndsu.edu/fileadmin/centers/americanindianhealth/files/History_and_Culture_Turtle_Mountain.pdf.

Roberts, Wynn. *My History with Remington Rand Through Unisys*. The VIP Club, March 13, 2011. http://vipclubmn.org/PeopleDocImg/OWRoberts.pdf.

Sarasohn, Homer. "First-Hand: Establishing Radio Communications in Post-WWII Japan." Engineering and Technology Wiki. Excerpted and adapted from "Japanese Students Have Surpassed U.S. Teachers," by Bart Ziegler, Associated Press, *Greenwich Times*, April 23, 1990. https://ethw.org/First-Hand:Establishing_Radio_Communications_in_Post-WWII_Japan.

Shelkey, Brenda. "On the Wings of a Prayer." *Underwood News* (Underwood, ND). November 12, 2009.

Spectrum. Fargo, ND. November 2, 1956.

State Historical Society of North Dakota. "Culture—Turtle Mountain."
    North Dakota Studies.
    https://www.ndstudies.gov/curriculum/high-school/turtle-
    mountain/culture-turtle-mountain.
Underwood, North Dakota. City of Underwood.
    http://www.underwoodnd.org.
VIP Club, The. "30-bit Computers." In *Information Technology (IT) Pioneers*,
    Chapter 52.
    http://vipclubmn.org/CP30bit.html.
Webb, Tom. "How St. Paul Was Almost Silicon Valley." *Twin Cities Pioneer
    Press*, January 2, 2010.
    https://www.twincities.com/2010/01/02/how-st-paul-
    was-almost-silicon-valley/.
Winegrad, Dilys and Atsushi Akera. "A Short History of the Second
    American Revolution." *University of Pennsylvania Almanac*, January 30,
    1996.
    https://almanac.upenn.edu/archive/v42/n18/eniac.html.

CPSIA information can be obtained
at www.ICGtesting.com
Printed in the USA
BVHW040719110922
646630BV00006B/16/J